# Cambridge Elements ☰

**Elements in Ethics**
edited by
Ben Eggleston
*University of Kansas*
Dale E. Miller
*Old Dominion University, Virginia*

# NATURAL LAW THEORY

Tom Angier
*University of Cape Town*

CAMBRIDGE
UNIVERSITY PRESS

# CAMBRIDGE
## UNIVERSITY PRESS

University Printing House, Cambridge CB2 8BS, United Kingdom

One Liberty Plaza, 20th Floor, New York, NY 10006, USA

477 Williamstown Road, Port Melbourne, VIC 3207, Australia

314–321, 3rd Floor, Plot 3, Splendor Forum, Jasola District Centre, New Delhi – 110025, India

103 Penang Road, #05–06/07, Visioncrest Commercial, Singapore 238467

Cambridge University Press is part of the University of Cambridge.

It furthers the University's mission by disseminating knowledge in the pursuit of education, learning, and research at the highest international levels of excellence.

www.cambridge.org
Information on this title: www.cambridge.org/9781108706391
DOI: 10.1017/9781108580793

First published 2021

*A catalogue record for this publication is available from the British Library.*

ISBN 978-1-108-70639-1 Paperback
ISSN 2516-4031 (online)
ISSN 2516-4023 (print)

# Natural Law Theory

Elements in Ethics

DOI: 10.1017/9781108580793
First published online: August 2021

Tom Angier
*University of Cape Town*

**Author for correspondence:** Tom Angier, tom.angier@uct.ac.za

**Abstract:** In Section 1, I outline the history of natural law theory, covering Plato, Aristotle, the Stoics and Aquinas. In Section 2, I explore two alternative traditions of natural law and explain why these constitute rivals to the Aristotelian tradition. In Section 3, I go on to elaborate a *via negativa* along which natural law norms can be discovered. On this basis, I unpack what I call three 'experiments in being', each of which illustrates the cogency of this method. In Section 4, I investigate and rebut two seminal challenges to natural law methodology, namely the fact/value distinction in metaethics and Darwinian evolutionary biology. In Section 5, I then outline and criticise the 'new' natural law theory, which is an attempt to revise natural law thought in light of the two abovementioned challenges. I conclude, in Section 6, with a summary and some reflections on the prospects for natural law theory.

This Element also has a video abstract: www.cambridge.org/angier

**Keywords:** natural law, Aristotle, Aquinas, teleology, Finnis, essentialism, naturalism

ISBNs: 9781108706391 (PB), 9781108580793 (OC)
ISSNs: 2516-4031 (online), 2516-4023 (print)

# Contents

1   Historical Introduction      1

2   'Natural Law' – Other Idioms      11

3   Some Experiments in Being      16

4   Two Core Challenges      23

5   'New' Natural Law      43

6   Prospective Conclusion      47

   References      49

# 1 Historical Introduction

Natural law theory has a rich and variegated history, richer and more variegated, perhaps, than that of other ethical theories in the Western tradition. This is because of its longevity and its predominance, moreover, until the early modern period. The idea that ethical norms, and specifically ethical laws or binding injunctions – whether of a positive or a negative (viz. prohibitory) kind – are grounded, ultimately, in nature (or, more specifically, in natural forms or essences) stretches back at least to Plato. It is in the Platonic dialogues that we encounter the notion that human conduct, if it is to be rightly ordered, must be *kata phusin*, that is, 'according to nature', or at least not *para phusin*, 'against nature'. The most explicit claims to this effect are put in the mouth of Callicles, who believes that 'nature itself reveals that it's a just thing for the better man and the more capable man to have a greater share than the worse and the less capable man' (*Gorgias* 483d). More explicitly, he holds that great military commanders like Xerxes act 'in accordance with the nature of what's just – yes, by Zeus, in accordance with the law of nature, and presumably not with the one we institute' (*Gorgias* 483e). Here we have the sophistic distinction between nature (*phusis*) and mere human law or convention (*nomos*),[1] but with the key innovation that human law is now properly subordinate and answerable to a law inscribed in nature. That is, we encounter, arguably for the first time, the idea that nature embodies not merely an array of systematically structured events and regularities, with no significance for human action, but also a definitive normative source, whose ends or purposes can be discovered and, indeed, must be discovered – and followed – in order that human life go well.[2]

Plato introduces the idea, then, that being 'according to nature' is not, primarily, what today would be called a purely factual or empirical or descriptive notion but something essentially normative and hence which bears intimately on practice.[3] This marks a break with the Sophists, for whom *nomos* and *phusis* were logically and metaphysically independent: 'law' pertaining exclusively to the human sphere, whereas 'nature' pertained to the whole world. The

---

[1] For the Sophists, viz. Socrates' main antagonists, nature operated in the same way throughout the *kosmos*, or world order, whereas law – construed as human, positive law – varied with particular cultures and their conventions. For more on the Sophists and the *nomos/phusis* distinction, see Barney (2006).

[2] Ironically, Callicles has often been labelled an 'immoralist'. Brian Leiter, for example, characterises Nietzsche as a devotee of 'Callicleanism', namely the doctrine that the strong or powerful should dominate the weak (see Leiter 2002, esp. 52–3, 145–6). The salient point here, however, is that, whatever the *content* of Calliclean norms, their *form* is that of natural law.

[3] NB Callicles: 'crowd-pleasing vulgarities that are admirable only by [human] law and not by nature' (*Gorgias* 482e); 'While Polus meant that doing it is more shameful by [human] law, you pursued the argument as though he meant by nature' (*Gorgias* 483a); 'all our [human] laws that violate nature' (*Gorgias* 484a).

trouble is that Plato offers no detailed, philosophical unpacking of *how* norms are grounded in nature. Worse, when it comes to the *Republic*, we are presented with a metaphysical theory that locates the ultimate source of all normativity in an entirely non-empirical, non-natural and transcendent realm, namely the realm of the Forms. In this way, Plato not only fails to elucidate the incipient idea of a natural law; he constructs a metaphysical framework which precludes ethical laws' having a natural foundation – as opposed to a natural embodiment – in the first place. As Hans Kelsen puts matters,

> The model after which positive law is to be fashioned – whether in general or individual norms – are not some norms immanent in the nature of empirical reality, but the idea of justice which is contained in the [Form] of the good . . . In its application to positive law Plato's doctrine of [Forms] is the exact opposite of a doctrine of natural law founded on observable facts of empirical reality. (Kelsen 1960: 64)

As a consequence, although Plato could be said to have inspired the Western tradition of natural law theory, he cannot be said to have initiated it.[4] Indeed, his commitment to what could be called 'normative transcendentalism' (or simply 'Platonism') placed a significant obstacle in its path. It fell to his student, Aristotle, to remove this obstacle.

Aristotle's great achievement, for our purposes, is to have taken seriously Plato's gestures toward a natural law while, simultaneously, not only dismantling Plato's normative transcendentalism but also replacing it with a naturalistic metaethics of his own.[5] This dismantling can be seen most directly in book 1, chapter 6 of the *Nicomachean Ethics* (*NE*), where Aristotle targets Plato's Form of the Good. In a series of quick-fire arguments, he accuses Plato of hypostatising a normative quality – namely, goodness – which does not belong properly in a transcendent realm, *qua* some absolutely superordinate entity, but functions rather as a relational property within the everyday, empirical world.[6] In short, goodness is, according to Aristotle, a normative quality immanent within things (or 'substances', *ousiai*) – to the degree, that is, they realise their specific form or essence. An acorn, for instance, has the form, essence or nature of an oak tree and is good – or 'perfect', 'complete', *teleios* – to the extent it realises or actualises that nature. An acorn that journeys toward maturity, therefore, but gets stunted in its development – owing (for example) to rocky ground or lack of

---

[4] Here I am in clear disagreement with John Wild's *Plato's Modern Enemies and the Theory of Natural Law* (Wild 1953), which argues that Plato propounds a genuine and systematic natural law ethics.

[5] Here I am in agreement with Edward Feser, who contrasts 'Platonic teleological realism' with 'Aristotelian teleological realism'. See Feser (2019b: 417). Cf. Oderberg (2007: 62–85).

[6] For a critique of the Platonic Form of the Good, along Aristotelian lines, see Williams (2003).

nourishment – is, *pro tanto*, defective or deficient or bad of its kind (albeit clearly through no 'fault' of its own). One that, by contrast, completes its journey to maturity, becoming a suitably tall, fruitful, adult oak tree, becomes as good as an oak tree can be. In this way, Aristotle's immanent, naturalistic conception of normativity is embedded in a network of interlocking metaphysical notions: notions such as matter and form, potentiality and actuality, essence and accident, natural function and natural end.[7] While these have their origin in Plato, they are endowed with conceptual clarity, determinacy and systematicity owing to Aristotle.

What has all this to do with natural law? Although Aristotle rarely refers explicitly to a 'natural law' or 'law of nature' (*nomos phuseôs*), he puts in place an ethical-cum-metaphysical conceptual scheme which, as I will explore further in what follows, is central to most subsequent natural law theory. At the heart of that scheme is the notion that norms are integral to nature, where nature is articulated through a series of (hierarchically arranged) species and where to each species there corresponds a natural function or *ergon*. As Aristotle elucidates in *NE* 1.7, at the bottom of the natural hierarchy there exists plant life,[8] with its relatively rudimentary (though often complex) vegetative modes of functioning. Above this, there exists animal life, which, although it incorporates various vegetative functions, adds other, higher functions, which afford the capacity both to perceive and to locomote; and above this, there exists human life, a type of animal life but one which adds to vegetation, perception and locomotion what Aristotle considers a unique mode of functioning within the animal kingdom: viz. rational (*logistikē*) functioning.[9] The latter depends on the presence of mind (*nous*), which has both practical and purely intellectual functions. The reason this hierarchy of life forms is salient for normativity is that, to each species, there is indexed a peculiar set of goods. A horse, for example, is completed or fulfilled differently to an acorn, while humans find their good in activities which depart from those subtending the good of horses. One could say, accordingly, that – for the Aristotelian – goodness is an *objective*

---

[7] For an elaboration of Aristotelian metaphysics, by scholars practised in anglophone analytic philosophy, see Oderberg (2007) and Feser (2014). For the application of Aristotelian metaphysics specifically to normativity, and more particularly to ethics (viz. normativity within the human realm), see Oderberg (2020). Central here is the idea of 'final' or end-directed explanation, the most salient among Aristotle's four 'causes' (*aitiai*).

[8] Aristotle speaks not of 'life' (*bios*) here but rather of 'soul' (*psuchē*). Owing, however, to the post-Cartesian conception of the soul as an immaterial, separate, mental substance, I think it less misleading to speak of 'life' in this context. ('Plant soul' verges on solecism, at least in modern English.)

[9] For Aristotle, human rationality is not unique *simpliciter*, since the divine is also rational (and supremely so). For the purposes of this Element, however, I will, as I explain in Section 2, bracket Aristotle's theology.

yet also an inescapably *relative* feature of living things: relative, that is, to their species essence.[10]

Now that we have gained a foothold, as it were, in Aristotle's metaphysics of goodness, it is time to look (as we did with Plato) at those passages within his work which refer most explicitly (and seminally) to natural law. While Aristotle, like Plato, speaks liberally of dispositions, actions and practices being *kata* or *para phusin*, that is, according to or against nature, he refers to 'natural law' as such only in *Rhetoric*, book 1, chapter 13. The passage in question is worth quoting at length, since it not only summarises Aristotle's view of natural law *per se*; it will also form the starting point of my own, constructive reflections on natural law in Section 3. It runs as follows:

> Particular law is that which each community lays down and applies to its own members: this is partly written and partly unwritten. Universal law is the law of nature. For there really is, as everyone to some extent divines, a justice and injustice that is naturally common [*phusei koinon*] to all, even to those who have no association or covenant with one another. It is this that Sophocles' Antigone clearly means when she says that the burial of Polyneices was a just act in spite of the prohibition: she means that it was just by nature. 'Not of today or yesterday it is, but lives eternal: none can date its birth'. And so Empedocles, when he bids us kill no living creature, says that doing this is not just for some people while unjust for others, 'Nay, but an all-embracing law, through the realms of the sky unbroken it stretcheth, and over the earth's immensity'. (*Rhetoric* 1.13, 1373b4–17)

Aristotle finishes with the claim that 'Alcidamas says the same in his Messeniac Oration', a gesture toward a view preserved by the scholiast, viz. that 'nature has made none a slave'. What does this passage, as a whole, tell us about Aristotle's conception of natural law?

First, he understands natural law as distinct from all positive or statute ('particular') law, because it is universal in its application. It holds, that is, between all humans, independently of any particular, contingent 'association' they may join or agreement they may draw up (see 1368b7–9). This is highlighted by Empedocles, who emphasises the 'all-embracingness' of natural law,

---

[10] Implicit here is the assumption that goodness – and badness, or in the older idiom, evil – inhabits or is inherent in the whole (at least living) world, not merely the human world. For those who assume (in line with the canons of anglophone analytic philosophy) that there are no *bona fide* values or norms beyond the sphere of human choice and practice, this appears odd. That value or normativity extends beyond the human sphere, however, is a key tenet of natural law theory, one to which I shall return. For more on the notion of objective yet relative goodness, see Martin (2008). (It is worth pointing out, in addition, that the relativity at stake here does not preclude a wider and deeper absolutism. For species-goods can be compared and themselves constitute an absolute hierarchy: a plant's life, for instance, is freighted with less intrinsic value than a human life – whatever condition they are in.)

suggesting it applies even beyond inter-human relations. Secondly, natural law is eternal and unchanging (cf. 1375a31–b2). Thirdly, Aristotle implies that natural law overrides, at least morally, any particular state law – its being universal and eternal indicates, in other words, its higher authority. This is reflected, notably, in Antigone's adherence to a natural justice that trumps the injustice (or, more specifically, impiety, viz. desecration of family duty) implicit in Creon's decree against burying her brother, Polyneices; and it is implied by Empedocles' metaphor of unimpeachable height, along with Alcidamas' bracing challenge to the ubiquitous institution of slavery. Along at least three dimensions, then – space, time and authority – Aristotle presents the natural law as superior to human-made or human-instituted law. It demonstrates an irrefragably wide spatio-temporal reach, which renders positive or particular law parochial by comparison. Furthermore, it is, by definition, superordinate to such law. Precisely because it is *not* formulated by humans – even though humans can grasp it – and, moreover, remains indelible within the nature of things, it has a claim on our respect which outstrips that of positive law.[11]

If this were all Aristotle had to say about natural law, one might place him at the inception of the natural law tradition. As with Plato, though, there are countervailing elements within his overall view. One reason to doubt he is a genuine natural law thinker lies in his markedly ambiguous attitude to the universality of the natural law. On the one hand, Aristotle views justice and friendship as coextensive, friendship existing 'by nature ... for those of the same kind as each other, and most of all for human beings, whence we praise "lovers of humans" (*philanthrōpoi*). And anyone could see on their travels how familiar (*oikeios*) and dear (*philos*) every human is to human' (*NE* 1155a16–22). He holds, moreover, that it is natural 'not to hunt human beings for food or sacrifice' (*Politics* 1324b22–41). On the other hand, Aristotle suggests that only (male) Greeks are fully human, and hence unfit for enslavement (*Politics* 1255a28–9); only Greek citizens are, for him, potential guest-friends, *xenoi* (*NE* 1161b11–16; cf. 1156a31). Furthermore, the mad and those he calls 'savages' (*thēriōdeis*) are excluded from ethical concern, and he tends to view many, if not all, barbarians (*barbaroi*, i.e. non-Greeks) as savages.[12] So, even if Aristotle maintains that the natural law is eternal and unchanging, real doubts surround his commitment to its universality; and if the normative content of positive or legal (or what in *NE* 5 he calls 'particular') justice not only happens but also ought to have force only within the borders of the Greek

---

[11] Not that positive law is somehow otiose for Aristotle. As he makes clear in *NE* 5, positive law is a valuable, necessary and central feature of a just state. It is rather that positive law is answerable, always and everywhere, to natural law, gaining its authority by conformity to the latter.

[12] See *NE* 1149a9–11, 1148b21–4; for *thēriōdēs* as a category, see 1145a17–33.

*polis* or city-state – and if, moreover, such justice not only has but also ought to have a highly restricted scope even within those borders – it seems that natural law's universality has, in Aristotle's work, little more than rhetorical force.[13]

I suggest, then, that there is a significant disparity between Aristotle's metaphysics on the one hand, which is manifold in its detail and proved highly influential on subsequent natural law theory, and his explicit reflections on natural law on the other, which are both disappointingly sparse and struggle to overcome internal inconsistency. True, in *NE* 5.7, Aristotle claims that political justice has two parts or aspects: one natural, the other conventional. As he contends,

> natural is what everywhere has the same power (*dunamis*), and not by being deemed so or not; conventional (*nomikos*) is what, to start with, makes no difference whether it is this way or that, but whenever they settle it, does make a difference. For example, to ransom at a mina, or to sacrifice a goat but not two sheep ... i.e. matters of decrees. (1134b19–24)

There is no evidence, however, that this invocation of 'natural' justice is a recapitulation of Aristotle's view in *Rhetoric* 1.13, to the effect that, as he puts it at *NE* 1134b24–5, 'that which is by nature is unchangeable and has everywhere the same force (as fire burns both here and in Persia)'. Instead, natural justice appears in this context to be merely intra-political, within the political community or *koinōnia*, and not, as in *Rhetoric*, trans-political; and this is because Aristotle is simply marking a (relatively uncontroversial) contrast between laws that don't need any (initially more or less arbitrary) practical specification and those that do.[14] This perfectly legitimate and intuitive contrast does not require a natural law that holds 'everywhere' – in the ambitious sense of 'in and for *any* community'.

So, although Aristotle does affirm certain practices as of universal value, and others of universal disvalue,[15] overall his theory of natural law remains *in nuce*.

---

[13] Aristotle might argue that only Greek citizen males qualify as fully human, and thus that only they count as full or proper subjects of justice. Indeed, this argument surfaces in his treatment of slavery, where he characterises slaves 'by nature' as rationally deficient and, consequently, as in need of a master (see *Politics* 1). This is widely acknowledged as a form of rationalisation, however (Aristotle's defence of 'natural' slavery is, it should be noted, in tension with *NE* 1161a32–b8, which distinguishes slave *qua* slave from slave *qua* human.) For Aristotle on slavery, see Deslauriers (2003), Heath (2008) and Leunissen (2017), esp. 53–7, 161–4.

[14] For example, refusing to support children when young or parents when old is ethically unacceptable for any Greek. By contrast, driving on the left or right is a matter of merely conventional justice (neither is intrinsically good and either is binding only when made a matter of law).

[15] An example of the former is Aristotle's 'polity', or mixed regime, whose constitution he characterises as best everywhere by nature (see *Politics* 4.11; cf. *NE* 5.7, *Politics* 7). Examples of the latter are adultery and theft (see *NE* 1107a8–12). Clearly, Aristotle does affirm virtue (*aretē*) as of universal value. Yet not only can *barbaroi* not instantiate the virtues; Aristotle rarely articulates virtuous conduct in terms of laws or rules (NB *NE* 2.2, 1103b34–104a11).

It is only with the Stoics that we find an explicitly and consistently cosmopolitan theory of natural law, in the literal sense that natural law norms have force beyond the Greek *polis* and apply, indeed, to the entire *kosmos*. Thus we find the Stoic Chrysippus asserting that 'There is no other or more appropriate way of approaching the theory of good and bad things or the virtues or happiness than from universal nature and from the administration of the world';[16] and Diogenes Laërtius holds that '"to live according to virtue" is equivalent to living according to the experience of events which occur by nature, as Chrysippus says in book 1 of his *On Goals* ... the goal becomes "to live consistently with nature", i.e. according to one's own nature and that of the universe'.[17] This un-Aristotelian emphasis on human nature as somehow enfolded within and answerable to cosmic nature goes along with another un-Aristotelian tendency, viz. a stress on moral law and, in particular, the 'common law' (*koinos nomos*). As Cicero reports the Stoic Laelius saying:

(1) True law is right reason, in agreement with nature, diffused over everyone, consistent, everlasting, whose nature is to advocate duty by prescription and to deter wrongdoing by prohibition ... (3) It is wrong to alter this law ... and it is impossible to abolish it entirely ... (4) There will not be a different law at Rome and at Athens, or a different law now and in the future, but one law, everlasting and immutable, will hold good for all peoples and at all times.[18]

With the Stoics, therefore, natural law theory comes into its own, entering a new and more dynamic phase. Gone is Aristotle's parochial attachment to the Greek *polis*, with its limited horizons, and gone is his sidelining of law as a foundational ethical notion.[19] The Stoics affirm a natural law explicitly and often and hold that its norms apply universally (with no groups falling short of full humanity). Equally, however, these gains are accompanied by certain losses. At a textual level, these consist in the fragmentary and largely second-hand nature of our evidence for Stoic doctrine. More pertinently, the Stoics do not build on or elaborate but tend to bracket the fine-grained metaphysical scheme that Aristotle had inherited from Plato and then carefully systematised.

---

[16] From his *Physical Postulates*. See Long and Sedley (1987: 368–9, fragment 60 A).

[17] From his *Lives of the Eminent Philosophers*. See Inwood and Gerson (2008: 114, fragment 88).

[18] From his *Republic*. See Long and Sedley (1987: 432–3, fragment 67 S). This passage is continuous with Cicero's frequent reference to a 'law of nature', or *lex naturalis*, most notably in *Concerning the Republic* (*De Re Publica*) and *Concerning the Laws* (*De Legibus*). See Cicero (1998).

[19] Aristotle spends much time in the *Politics* on positive law, and in *NE* 5 he articulates the virtue of justice partly in terms of rules of 'equality' (*isonomia*). When it comes to his ethical theory, though, he places virtue front and centre, with laws, rules and norms of practice playing an inconspicuous and subordinate role.

Largely absent, in other words, are concepts like essence, potentiality, species and genus, prime matter and substantial form. It is as if the Stoics' theoretical reliance on a cosmic or common nature (*phusis koinē*), together with their foregrounding of a 'law' commensurate with that nature, serves more or less to displace Aristotle's focus on different orders of natural being, along with his detailed unpacking of their metaphysical infra- and superstructure. In this way, the Stoics' demonstrably more adequate recognition of the natural law's universality comes at the expense of Aristotle's hard-won metaphysical sophistication. Indeed, the Stoics forgo the latter only to replace it with a comparatively coarse-grained and implausible conceptual scheme. How so?

What I have in mind here, primarily, is the way the Stoics treat nature, (right) reason, God (or Zeus) and even virtue as substantially interchangeable concepts. Take, for instance, the continuation of the above-cited passage from Diogenes Laertius:

> Thus Zeno first, in his book *On Human Nature*, said that the goal was to live in agreement with nature, which is to live according to virtue ... doing nothing which is forbidden by the common law, which is right reason, penetrating all things, being the same as Zeus, who is the leader of the administration of things. And this itself is the virtue of the happy man and a smooth flow of life, whenever all things are done according to the harmony of the *daimōn* in each of us with the will of the administrator of the universe.[20]

Or take Cicero:

> Law is the highest reason, implanted in Nature, which commands what ought to be done and forbids the opposite ... the origin of Justice is to be found in Law, for Law is a natural force; it is the mind and reason of the intelligent man. (*De Legibus* 1.18–19)

Or as Plutarch quotes Chrysippus:

> one can find no other starting point for justice except the one derived from Zeus and that derived from the common nature ... there is no other, and certainly no more appropriate, way to approach the discussion of good and bad things or the virtues or happiness, [except] on the basis of common nature and the administration of the cosmos.[21]

Admittedly, this conceptual lability stems from Stoic doctrine, which holds that nature is identical to God, God is tantamount to his reason and virtue reduces to the practical exercise of reason. Yet it is precisely this series of elisions – or at

---

[20] From his *Lives of the Eminent Philosophers*. See Inwood and Gerson (2008: 114, fragment 88).
[21] From his *On Stoic Self-Contradictions*. See Inwood and Gerson (1997: 253, fragment II-113).

least what appear such, from a Platonic or Aristotelian perspective – which renders that doctrine insufficiently informative.[22]

It is only with Thomas Aquinas, in the thirteenth century, that the Platonic, Aristotelian and Stoic contributions to natural law theory are fully synthesised, and to vastly influential effect. The *locus classicus* of Aquinas' analysis of natural law is *Summa Theologiae* I–II, question 94. Like the Stoics, he avoids Aristotle's ambiguity over the universality of natural law. Indeed, in article 4, entitled 'Whether the Natural Law Is the Same in All Men?', he argues, in detail, that 'The natural law is common to all nations'. He qualifies this claim, however, by maintaining that, although 'the natural law, as to general principles, is the same for all, both as to rectitude and as to knowledge ... as to certain matters of detail, which are conclusions, as it were, of those general principles ... in some few cases it may fail'.[23] The reasons for this 'failure' are that, as to 'rectitude' (i.e. normative content), a practically rational principle may have exceptions in certain circumstances (e.g. one should return borrowed goods, but not if they will be used for purposes of sedition); while, as to knowledge, the natural law may be obscured by passions or evil habits. In article 5 – entitled 'Whether the Natural Law Can Be Changed?' – Aquinas affirms the eternality of the natural law, though here, too, he enters qualifications. One of these is that, through God's command, 'certain detailed proximate conclusions drawn from the first principles [of natural law]' may be changed in specific cases – for instance, taking (what appears) someone else's property ceases to be theft, if God designates it to be taken.[24] Further, in article 6 – entitled 'Whether the Law of Nature Can Be Abolished from the Heart of Man?' – Aquinas argues that the natural law is indelible as to its first and most general precepts but not as to its secondary and derived precepts, which can be rendered obscure (once again, by passion or habit).

From this brief outline, it is clear that, in at least one, foundational, respect, Aquinas' theory of natural law marks a radical departure from the Graeco-Roman theories we have looked at so far. This departure consists not in the fact that Aquinas' theory is embedded in a theistic framework: Plato, Aristotle and

---

[22] Hegel makes a similar criticism of Stoicism in his *Phenomenology of Spirit*: 'The True and the Good', he writes, 'wisdom and virtue, the general terms beyond which Stoicism cannot get, are ... in a general way no doubt uplifting, but since they cannot in fact produce any expansion of the content, they soon become tedious' (Hegel 1977: 122, §200). (I thank Robert Stern for this reference.) For conspectuses of the Stoics on natural law, see Klein (2012) and Brüllmann (2019).

[23] It is worth noting that, for Aquinas, the first and most basic principle of practical reason is 'the good is to be done and pursued, and evil is to be avoided'. This foundational principle is absolute and unchangeable. For a seminal paper on the 'first principle of practical reason', see Grisez (1965).

[24] Cf. Simon (1965: 146–7) and Crowe (1977: 285).

the Stoics are, after all, theists (albeit of different stripes).[25] It consists, rather, in the fact that Aquinas is a monotheist and, more particularly, a Judaeo-Christian monotheist. He is writing, moreover, within a tradition of fine-grained philosophical theology, which, however rigorous in its philosophical method, presupposes strong theological axioms – hence his two most seminal works are entitled *Summa Theologiae* ('Treatise on Theology') and *Summa contra Gentiles* ('Treatise against the Gentiles'). What follows at the level of substantive theory is that Aquinas must not only deny the pantheism of the Stoics but also repudiate the vague, retiring theism of Plato and Aristotle, who refer (seemingly indifferently) to both 'god' (*theos*) and 'gods' (*theoi*). Aquinas' God is a God who, unlike the god of the Stoics, transcends the world and, unlike the divinity of Aristotle, is a personal God who issues commands and gets involved directly in human life (not by attracting people merely as an impersonal object of love).[26] While Aquinas' God is, like humans, rational, His rationality is of a transcendent – and hence, in significant ways, unknowable – order. Indeed, because of this, and because of God's omnipotence, Aquinas envisages Him as intervening in the human, moral, order in ways alien to and perhaps unintelligible for Greek or Roman philosophers.

When it comes to the *structure* of Aquinas' natural law theory, it is, by contrast, thoroughly indebted to the Greeks, and especially to Aristotle's hierarchical and essentialist conception of living species. Indeed Acquinas presents human nature, and the goods to which it is ordered, as a rational summation and completion of the natural functions – both vegetative and animal – found in lower species. Thus, as he explains in the pivotal *Summa Theologiae* I–II, question 94, article 2:

> in man there is first of all an inclination (*inclinatio*) to good in accordance with the nature which he has in common with all substances: inasmuch as every substance seeks the preservation of its own being, according to its nature: and by reason of this inclination, whatever is a means of preserving human life, and of warding off its obstacles, belongs to the natural law. Secondly, there is in man an inclination to things that pertain to him more specially, according to that nature which he has in common with other animals: and in virtue of this inclination, those things are said to belong to the natural law, 'which nature has taught to all animals', such as sexual intercourse, education of offspring and so forth. Thirdly, there is in man an inclination to good, according to the nature of his reason, which nature is proper to him: thus man has a natural inclination to know the truth about God, and to live in society: and in this respect, whatever pertains to this inclination

---

[25] For an argument that Aristotle is closer to Aquinas in this respect than usually recognised, see Angier (2019).

[26] For more detail on Aristotle's theism, see Mirus (2004, 2012).

belongs to the natural law; for instance, to shun ignorance, to avoid offending those among whom one has to live, and other such things regarding the above inclination.

The metaphysical profile of Aquinas' notion of 'natural inclinations' is disputed, especially since they are not mentioned, as such, by Aristotle.[27] What is clear, however, is that their *content* follows that propounded in Aristotle's species-hierarchy. Hence the most basic inclination is to life, which is shared with all living things; then there is the inclination to procreation and the rearing of young, which is shared with all animals; and finally, there is the specifically human inclination to rational goods, both practical and theoretical (or 'speculative'), the latter including the good of knowing about God. This completes, in summary form, Aquinas' articulation of the natural law and its grounding in human nature.[28] Before elaborating and defending my own raft of natural law goods and their respective grounds (in Section 3), I need to unpack what senses of 'natural law' I will not be addressing in this Element and why.

## 2 'Natural Law' – Other Idioms

If Aquinas represents the full flowering of natural law theory in its Christianised (yet philosophically, still substantively Greek) form, this hardly meant the end of such theory in the West. Not only does Thomistic natural law continue as a tradition in its own right;[29] Aristotelian moral metaphysics was subsumed also within the Jewish and Muslim traditions.[30] After the mediaeval period, however, there developed a tradition of purportedly 'natural law' thought with which I will not be concerned in this Element. The main representatives of this tradition are Hobbes, Locke and Rousseau, viz. the early modern 'social contract' theorists, who put natural law on a wholly new footing – one incompatible with the tradition which has its roots in the Greeks and reaches its culmination in Aquinas. Wherefore this marked incompatibility, and even rivalry?

The early modern social contract conception of natural law is fundamentally at odds with the tradition I have outlined, primarily owing to its profound reconstrual and reconfiguration of 'nature'. The classical and mediaeval tradition understands nature in teleological and essentialist terms, that is, as I have

---

[27] For an excellent introduction to Aquinas on natural inclinations, see Jensen (2019). It is vital not to conflate Aquinas' *inclinationes* with mere impulses or desires. The latter are transitory and vary with each individual, whereas the former are constitutive of human nature and its most profound modes of fulfilment.

[28] For more detailed treatments, see Lisska (1996), Goyette et al. (2004) and Jensen (2015).

[29] See, for example, Maritain (2001), Porter (2005), Di Blasi (2006) and Alford (2010).

[30] For introductions to both, see Rudavsky (2019) and Emon (2019), respectively. I will tackle generically theological approaches to natural law theory further on in this section.

argued, as an array of species, each with its own essence, where each is directed or ordered to its own, peculiar end, which is tantamount to its proper good.[31] In the human case, this involves being ordered to live in society, since humans are what Aristotle calls 'political animals' (*zôia politica*), whose essence is fundamentally social. That is, they are the kind of animals, who, in contrast to (say) orangutans, are fitted to and fulfilled by living with one another. The first society they inhabit is the family, but as they mature, they find their place in larger social groupings, which exist partly in order to supply needs which could not be supplied by smaller ones. A key corollary of this is that properly functioning humans must develop the virtues, viz. those traits which (among other things) undergird and sustain relatively large-scale social life.[32] This is, once again, not against their nature, since – as Aristotle puts things – human beings are 'fitted by nature to receive' the virtues (*NE* 1103a23–5). Responsible parents and States will, therefore, inculcate the virtues in their young, since this is not only for their individual good but also for the common good. In this way, the teleological essentialism of traditional natural law never questions humans' basic sociability, whether at the level of family or political life. It thus understands the State as a 'natural' form, outside of which humans, as they are constituted, cannot survive (or at least cannot survive well).[33]

By contrast, 'natural law', in its paradigm early modern acceptation, understands human nature as ordered to social and political life only accidentally. On its view, the defining feature of human nature is the pursuit of self-interest, so that society appears not as the natural context within which humans exist and flourish but rather as a solution, *faute de mieux*, for those seeking to satisfy their individual wants and desires; and this metaphysical reconfiguration brings with it, in turn, a new conceptual scheme, which, although it contains the concept 'nature', lends the latter radically new content. According to Hobbes, for

---

[31] For the teleological and essentialist character of traditional natural law, see Oderberg (2010: 59–64) and Oderberg (2013: 376). Cf. Simon (1965: 42–3, 52–3, 121); Maritain (2001: 27–8, 36–7); Donnelly (2006: 8, 10, 12); Spaemann (2008: 293–4).

[32] I do not mean to suggest that the nature or value of the virtues is exhausted by their social function; but they do have this function, in addition to *per se* or intrinsic value. (NB even a consequentialist like Thomas Hurka argues that virtue has intrinsic value; see Hurka 2001.)

[33] NB 'he who is unable to live in society, or who has no need because he is sufficient for himself, must be either a beast or a god: he is no part of a State' (*Politics* 1.2, 1253a28–30). Christof Rapp argues for the naturalness of the State in precisely this way, viz. that it reflects the nature and hence proper ordering of its human constituents (see Rapp 2016). It might be objected that the Christian ideal of the hermitic life is left out of account here. Yet not only are hermits necessarily socialised within human communities; the purpose of the hermitic life is not to deny or depreciate the good of community but rather (in part) to pray for its moral purity and integrity – human communities being subject to perennial corruption and temptation. (It is worth adding that the rationale of eremitism presupposes revelation, which, as I will go on to explore, lies beyond the justificatory resources of natural law *stricto sensu*.)

instance, the 'state of nature' is a social condition, prior to any State structures or the enforcement of law; it is not something, therefore, which is dynamic or aspirational but rather something to be escaped, being the limiting case of insecurity and anarchy. Rousseau inverts this picture, with nature encapsulating a kind of prelapsarian condition, in which people exist uncorrupted by the depredations of civil society, a condition supposedly instantiated (as in Hobbes) before the development of the State. Despite Rousseau's axiological inversion, then, Hobbes's notion that nature is something wholly non-dynamic, and captured by a pre-existing state of things, is preserved; and given this reconstrual, 'nature' takes on either a wholly negative valence (as for Hobbes) or a wholly positive valence (as for Rousseau) – but on either construal, it ceases to embody any intrinsic teleology or orderedness, whereby those acting 'according to nature' move from a state of immaturity to maturity, from incompletion to fulfilment. Nature becomes something merely to leave behind or to recover in its entirety.[34] It is hence static and monotonic.

Much more could be said about the innovations of the early moderns, including their unprecedented moves in the theories of sovereignty, governance and moral psychology. Yet suffice it to say that, for our purposes, their theoretical departures represent – for the advocate of traditional natural law – a 'great unlearning'. This stems, at root, from their rejection of Aristotelian metaphysics, with its commitment to nature *qua* panoply of interrelated essences, each with its own, specific teleology. Heinrich Rommen is correct, in this sense, to characterise the early modern natural lawyers as 'metaphysicophobic',[35] even if their pared-down, deflationary, conception of human nature and its powers does constitute a metaphysics of a sort. One way of capturing this contrast is to characterise traditional natural law as resting on a *lex ratio*, whereas social contract natural law rests on a *lex voluntas*.[36] That is, traditional natural law understands reason as discerning norms in nature, and the individual will as 'measured' by these,[37] whereas early modern natural law comes to rest on the individual will as such, which is intrinsically unstructured and determined primarily on its own survival. Another way of capturing this contrast is to oppose a fundamentally social and relational conception of human nature to

---

[34] For more on early modern natural law theory, see Rommen (1998: ch. 4). On the 'state of nature', in particular, see Rommen (1998: 21, 38–9, 68, 193) and Manent (2018: 8–12). I leave Locke to one side, because his notion of the state of nature is less starkly amoral than Hobbes's, even though the grounds for the 'natural laws' he posits remain obscure.

[35] See Rommen (1998: 142 n. 1); cf. Rommen (1998: 80, 85, 105, 114, 117–18, 141, 150).

[36] See Rommen (1998: 36, 51, 54, 70); cf. Simon (1965: 61, 80, 174–5).

[37] For the natural law as, in Aquinas' sense, the 'rule and measure' of human acts, see Maritain (2001: 32) and Simon (1965: 71).

a fundamentally individualistic and atomistic one.[38] Both these modes of contrast have their merits, despite my somewhat crude and summary descriptions of them. The crucial point here, though, is that traditional natural law – which, philosophically, is an essentially Graeco-Roman artefact – remains incompatible with its early modern namesake, embodying an essentially rival set of assumptions and conclusions (which are, moreover, false – as Section 3 will hopefully bring out).[39] From now on, I will focus exclusively on the former.

The second approach to natural law theory I will adumbrate, but not pursue, could be called 'theological'. A paradigm case of this approach is that of David Novak, the Jewish natural law theorist.[40] According to Novak, only a 'theologically formulated' natural law theory can be both well-founded and persuasive (Novak 2014: 6). At the very least, 'theistically cogent natural law theory can be shown', he holds, 'to be more cogent than its ancient Greek or modern ... rivals' (Novak 2014: 7–8). By 'theologically formulated' or 'theistically cogent', he means a form of natural law that appeals, and appeals centrally, to revealed texts: in his case, the *Tanakh* or Hebrew Bible. The latter supplies the key premises for Novak's natural law argument, premises that could not be supplied by the purely immanent or non-transcendent data afforded by traditional natural law.[41] A parallel theological approach is advocated by Jean Porter, though in her case the revelation at issue is Christian.[42] According to Porter, a purely philosophical approach to natural law fails to yield universal, detailed, practical norms. The latter can be arrived at, she maintains, only once the content of revelation is taken into account. As she puts matters, 'even on the most optimistic showing, any attempt to specify the general precepts of the natural law will remain indeterminate and incomplete, apart from the traditions and practices of some specific community. In particular, the natural law as we Christians understand and formulate it will inevitably involve some degree of theological specification'.[43]

---

[38]  See Rommen (1998: ch. 4) and Manent (2018: 21–3).

[39]  The rivalry at issue is nicely brought out by Knud Haakonssen: 'On the one hand', he writes, 'natural law theory sustained the continuous development of a metaphysically based realism and objectivism as the dominant force in moral theory from late scholasticism to the 19th century. On the other hand, natural law in an entirely different vein, that of voluntarism ... simultaneously provided all the elements of an anti–metaphysical conventionalism in morals' (Haakonssen 2008: 147).

[40]  See, especially, Novak (1998, 2014).

[41]  God does play *some* role in traditional natural law – according to Aquinas, as the creator of nature and 'promulgator' of the natural law – but not God's revealed will, or the data of revelation more widely. I shall come back to this contrast in the next paragraph.

[42]  See, especially, Porter (1999, 2005). For references to and defences of her theological approach, see Porter (2005: 5, 134–6).

[43]  Porter (2009: 91). Similar positions are expressed in Dubois (2006: 194), Wildes (2006: 38) and Levering (2008).

Svend Andersen labels this approach 'theological unificationism', that is, 'the effort of integrating philosophical ethics into the framework of theological ethics'.[44] The trouble with this approach is manifold; I will highlight only three problems with it. First, it rests on premises that appeal to, and are perhaps intelligible, only to those already part of a particular faith community and tradition. Hence, whatever their significant overlap, Novak's selection of revelatory texts and Porter's equivalent set have necessarily limited appeal (and even limited intelligibility) in any forum that admits atheists or theists from other traditions. Secondly, by placing central and essential weight on divine revelation, theological unificationists set great store by claims which are metaphysically strongly controverted.[45] So on both epistemological and metaphysical grounds, their approach looks highly costly and relatively unpropitious. Thirdly, these systemic drawbacks are underscored by the historical fact that even philosophical theologians like Aquinas are not theological unificationists when it comes to the natural law. True, Aquinas assumes that the natural law participates in eternal and divine law, and that it is binding partly in virtue of such participation, but this is consistent with Aquinas' further view that the *content* of natural law is independent of revelation,[46] and, indeed, that its value is largely owing to this independence (non-believers are equally subject to it and, moreover, equally capable of discerning it).[47] So on the three grounds I have just outlined – epistemological, metaphysical and historical – I will, from now on, be putting aside the theological approach to natural law theory.[48]

---

[44] See Andersen (2001: 351–2).

[45] Granted, some will maintain that Aristotelian–Thomistic metaphysics is no less controversial – especially with respect to its essentialism and natural teleology. That is why I will spend Section 4 defending it, particularly with regard to its rejection of the fact/value distinction and its relation to Darwinian evolutionary biology. If my arguments there are sound, Aristotelian–Thomistic metaphysics has – at least *pro tanto*, and as deployed within natural law theory – nothing to fear from its critics.

[46] NB S. Adam Seagrave: 'St. Thomas's natural law is truly "natural", that is, not dependent in the order of knowledge on the eternal law or the Divine Reason from which the eternal law emanates. Since the eternal law is reflected in the objective order within and among created beings, including the human being, all that is required for understanding the first principles of the natural law is the intellectual procedure of induction from objective reality' (Seagrave 2009: 519).

[47] Cf. David Oderberg, who holds that, even though the world order requires a divine orderer (see Oderberg 2010: 48–51, 54, 57), one can deny (or at least ignore) God's role in creating the natural law without 'epistemic vice'. As he writes: 'one can, and people often do, recognise a natural purpose or function in things without giving the slightest attention to the distinct question of whether that purpose or function is bestowed by an extrinsic principle' (Oderberg 2010: 63). Cf. Feser on 'scholastic teleological realism' (Feser 2015: 35).

[48] For a historically rich and sympathetic treatment of this theological approach within the Catholic tradition, see Rowland (2019).

## 3 Some Experiments in Being

Having outlined the broad structure of traditional natural law theory (in Section 1),
then indicated its main competitors (in Section 2), I want now to explore natural
law theory as a substantive method with its own deliverances.[49] As to method,
I could rest content with reiterating the Aristotelian normative metaphysics
I elaborated in Section 1.[50] It is more fruitful, for present purposes, however, to
take a different approach – one used, as I will explicate below, by early twenty-first-
century political philosophers. Not only is this alternative method intuitive and
minimally demanding metaphysically; it also reflects that *Urtext* of natural law
thought, Sophocles' *Antigone*.[51] Once I have unpacked both the natural law
implications of *Antigone* and the incipient philosophical method to which they
point, I will go on to use this method, myself, to develop (what I will call) some
'experiments in being'. These will constitute a brief series of vignettes designed
both to 'update' the practical lessons of *Antigone* and to illustrate the cogency of
Sophocles' implicit method.[52] In this way, I hope to vindicate – or, at the very least,
to carve out a legitimate space for – natural law-type reasoning, along with the
practical conclusions which it supports; and this not in the promissory way
suggested by John Stuart Mill's merely notional 'experiments in living' but rather
in a concrete, determinate and hopefully more convincing manner.[53]

To start, then, with *Antigone*: why does Aristotle identify Sophocles' tragic
drama as a foundational natural law text, and why does Jacques Maritain refer to
Antigone herself as a 'heroine of natural law' (Maritain 2001: 26)? In order to
answer these questions, we need to outline the drama in its philosophical
lineaments.[54] Antigone, the daughter of Oedipus, has two brothers – Eteocles
and Polyneices – who, prior to the drama, have fought to the death for the
kingship of Thebes. Neither survives. Creon, who assumes the kingship, decides
that Eteocles deserves to be buried but that Polyneices – because he led a foreign
army – should be left to rot on the battlefield. Antigone refuses to accept this

---

[49] I am narrowing my purview here to the core – i.e. teleological and perfectionistic – aspects of that
    method. Natural law theory also encompasses work on moral rightness, moral principles, virtue
    and rights. To address all of these would be unwieldy, however. Crucially, and as I hope my
    'experiments in being' suggest, claims about rightness, principles and virtue all find their
    ultimate grounding and intelligibility in objective human goods.

[50] For particularly clear, erudite, modern, expressions of this method – which, nonetheless, do not
    enter into the complex (and sometimes rarefied) detail found in scholars like Feser, Mirus and
    Oderberg – see Veatch (1966, 2003) and Hüntelmann (2016).

[51] See Aristotle's *Rhetoric* 1.13, 1373b4–17 in Section 1.

[52] Without denying, that is, the well-foundedness of *Antigone*'s original lessons. I want simply to
    supply further examples – ones that recommend themselves more intuitively, perhaps, to
    a modern audience.

[53] For Mill's idea of 'experiments in living' (or 'experiments of living'), see *On Liberty* (Mill
    1985), esp. ch. 3 ('On Individuality, as One of the Elements of Well-Being').

[54] See Sophocles (1954).

decree and proceeds to bury Polyneices herself. This sets in train a series of tragic events, precipitated by Creon's refusal to heed Tiresias the prophet, who declares the justice of Antigone's action. Antigone is exiled, then hangs herself, leading Haemon (her fiancé and Creon's son) to suicide, and thence to the suicide of Eurydice, Creon's wife. This calamitous series of events stands as a reproach to Creon, who ends up bereft of his family, precisely in virtue of having refused Antigone the right to fulfil her family duty, viz. to bury her brother. The plot thus dramatises a conflict between those who think that 'the men in power' (l. 67) can legitimately and definitively set the laws and those who think there is a higher law or set of norms, to which those in authority are subordinate. In this way, there is some analogy with the conflict between Thrasymachus and Socrates in book 1 of Plato's *Republic*: for Thrasymachus believes that 'justice is the advantage of the stronger', that is, it exists to serve those who happen to be in power at the time. Even if Creon has *some* right on his side – after all, he is trying to restore a social order ripped apart by civil war – he abuses his power by insisting that a defeated enemy has no entitlements, even in death.

The conflict Sophocles dramatises is articulated, philosophically, largely in terms of virtue and virtuous action. Creon stands against that modality of justice called 'piety', viz. the virtue of honouring one's family. As Antigone puts it, 'It's not for him to keep me from my own' (l. 48): 'Friend shall I lie with him [viz. Polyneices], yes friend with friend, when I have dared the crime of piety' (ll. 73–4). This brings out nicely the fact that, under Creon's regime, virtuous action is liable to constitute a (legal, not moral) crime. It also brings out how, when characterising what is natural, in the Aristotelian sense, one cannot adequately *describe* what is happening without employing inextricably *evaluative* terms. One cannot get a grip, in other words, on Creon's character or actions without seeing them as (by extension) impious: in the sense that they prevent Antigone from fulfilling what is due to her family. On the one hand, Creon's rhetoric is replete with references to the State and its supposed exigencies. He declares, for example, that 'The man who is well-minded to the State from me in death and life shall have his honour' (ll. 209–10); 'No current custom among men as bad as silver currency. This destroys the State' (ll. 296–7); 'This girl was expert in her insolence when she broke bounds beyond established law' (ll. 480–1). On the other hand, this blinds him to the vital quality of those bonds which characterise that first and most intimate of human associations, the family. As he avers, 'She is my sister's child, but were she child of closer kin than any at my hearth, she and her sister should not so escape their death and doom' (ll. 486–9).[55]

---

[55] It is worth highlighting that Antigone is not asserting, in and through her words and actions, that Polyneices was politically or morally in the right. She is committed, merely, to the view that one should afford one's family members an honourable burial. (Cf. Euthyphro, who thinks that piety

In terms of philosophical method and its purchase for natural law theory, Sophocles' *Antigone* points the way to two key features. First, natural law norms can, and perhaps can best, be discerned when they are disrespected or contravened. That is, we are alerted to and come to appreciate the value of piety not by the mere enunciation of piety as a virtue, or by having a character preach that pious actions are good. Rather, piety is revealed as a category of good to which humans are essentially ordered precisely by the active frustration and denial of that good. Put otherwise, it seems the most effective way of uncovering the natural law is along the *via negativa*, which demonstrates what the world is like when that law is no longer honoured in people's thoughts and actions.[56] Second, the mode of this dishonouring is not at the relatively abstract level of principle or rule or norm. For none of Sophocles' characters directly or explicitly condemns justice or piety. Rather, the contravention is made apparent at the level of particular actions: Antigone insists on burying Polyneices, and it is this, particular, action that Creon strenuously opposes. It follows that the natural law is being signalled, primarily, in a bottom-up way, by experience of and reflection on particular, highly textured actions, which render vivid what it means at the level of *concrete being* to contravene a norm that might appear, otherwise, to have little foothold in the actual world. This negative, indirect and concrete mode of investigating the natural law need not, moreover, be merely *faute de mieux*, but may, as I shall now argue, constitute a proper and effective way of manifesting natural law norms.

In order to argue for this, I want to take a brief detour into political philosophy and, specifically, the theory of 'social equality'. Social egalitarians have themselves faced the problem of identifying which norms are definitive of their position, and with instructive results for natural law. The work of Jonathan Wolff is especially helpful here.[57] Wolff contends that '[f]or those who defend social equality, the lack of a clear positive model of a society of equals may appear to be a significant problem, in urgent need of remedy. And yet there is another perspective we could take' (Wolff 2015: 215). Wolff finds this alternative perspective in the work of Amartya Sen, whose *The Idea of Justice* (Sen 2009) advocates not a positive model of justice (as found, paradigmatically, in John Rawls) but rather a negative approach, which identifies the various

---

requires prosecuting his father for manslaughter, yet who no doubt also believes him worthy of an honourable burial. See Plato's early dialogue, *Euthyphro*.)

[56] Granted, Sophocles portrays this world in dramatic mode, so that Creon's contravention of the natural law generates catastrophic consequences that would not normally arise. Yet the usual absence of such overtly dire consequences does not detract from the integrity or well-foundedness of Sophocles' vision. He is merely showing Creon's destructive attitude to the natural law by embodying it *in foro externo*.

[57] See Wolff (2015).

injustices that exist in the world. As Wolff puts matters: 'the task for political philosophers is to identify manifest injustice and to work out how those injustices can be overcome' (Wolff 2015: 215). Calling this the 'manifest injustice thesis', Wolff adds that '[m]ethodologically, the advantage for social egalitarians of Sen's observation is clear. What appeared to be a defect – the lack of a clear positive account of social equality – turns out to be no such thing. Social egalitarians can have a clear sense of what they are against – hierarchy, snobbery, servility, oppression – and this is all that is needed' (Wolff 2015: 216).

Wolff then explores several challenges to this *via negativa*. Centrally, he considers whether injustice is 'failure to measure up to a standard, and any judgement of injustice relies on an account of justice' (Wolff 2015: 217). This challenge rests on the claim that 'one can only know the negative by knowing the positive ... the epistemological thesis itself ... likely ... [being] based on a claim of conceptual or logical priority' (Wolff 2015: 218). Wolff goes on, however, to dispute both the challenge and the claims on which it rests – citing two basic reasons. First, in Stuart Hampshire's words, 'My political opinions and loyalties, when challenged ... [need not] include or entail any generalisable account of a future ideal society or of essential human virtues. Rather, they point [...] to the possible elimination of particular evils found in particular societies at particular times, and not to universalisable principles of social justice' (Hampshire 2000: x). This logical reason (resting on a claim of non-entailment) is complemented by a second, explanatory reason, viz. that 'when we look at forms of social organisation that we might describe as egalitarian, it is not at all clear that they have much in common rather than avoiding certain forms of divisions ... [or] certain types of asymmetric social relations. And it would ... be hard to argue that one of these provides the sole template for a society of equals' (Wolff 2015: 221). In other words, the successful identification of 'manifest injustices' – in this case, manifest social inequalities – does not require the possession (or even the existence) of a single, positive, univocal and systematic conception of social equality. Indeed, such identification is consistent with a plurality of such conceptions, or even none at all.

I am sceptical whether these logically and explanatorily highly deflationary claims have application, *mutatis mutandis*, to natural law. I would argue that the existence of manifest natural evils *does* entail (some or other) positive natural law theory, and that such a theory *must* hold for those evils to be evil in the first place.[58] The key issue for present purposes, however, is neither logical nor

---

[58] In brief, my argument depends on separating Wolff's epistemological thesis, which is well-founded, from his logical and explanatory theses, which are ill-founded. In other words, although we can discover natural law norms by the *via negativa*, the latter remains a purely epistemic method, so cannot justify those norms or supply them with ultimate grounds.

explanatory – but epistemic. For whether or not a positive theory of natural law exists (or can, moreover, be discovered), I would contend that manifest natural evils are highly propitious when it comes to displaying and realising the cogency of natural law norms. As Wolff might put it (following G. A. Cohen), whether or not there exists a positive 'currency' (Wolff 2015: 221) of natural law,[59] the *via negativa* is a consummately useful method with which to feel our way toward those modes of action natural law definitively rejects, impugns, recommends or enjoins absolutely. This is, indeed, precisely the method evidenced, artistically, by Sophocles' *Antigone*, and precisely that aspect of Wolff's 'manifest injustice thesis' which carries weight. So our immediate task is to get a firm sense of or grip on the *range* of manifest natural evils – however, exactly, these are structured and explained at the level of theory. Once we have worked our way through these 'experiments in being', we will be in a position to judge what light they throw, retrospectively, on the Aristotelian metaphysics I outlined in Section 1.

The first of my three 'experiments in being' concerns the most basic form of natural evil, namely that which undermines and infringes on human vegetative functioning. Take a person, S, who, having led a relatively normal life, is put in a confined space – a couple of underground rooms, say, with no windows – and is fed a diet that is nutritionally rudimentary, at best. Not only is S deprived compared to their previous life; they are deprived absolutely, since human beings are not ordered to a life that is so constricted in terms of movement, natural light and nutrition. S will do badly, not merely in virtue of having their desires frustrated but objectively and whether or not their desires are frustrated. They are being subjected to living conditions that are detrimental to them, whether they know it or not, and whether they care or not. Furthermore, it would be misleading to say that the depredations they suffer are simply 'biological'. Rather, we judge, and judge correctly, that when S suffers thus in their biological being, they are suffering themselves, intimately and personally (however 'basic' the functions that are being frustrated); and this points up a wider fact: that in order to describe S's situation accurately and fully, there is no possibility of circumventing evaluative language. We are inclined to say, for instance, that S's condition is manifestly one of deprivation, hardship and want: these descriptions having inextricably evaluative content. If one tried, moreover, to characterise S's condition in purely non-evaluative language, one would find oneself drawing on not only a highly restricted vocabulary but also one constitutionally incapable of expressing the reality one confronts.[60]

---

[59] Wolff is borrowing here from G. A. Cohen's paper, 'On the Currency of Egalitarian Justice' (Cohen 1989).

[60] Likewise, it would be very awkward, artificial and, indeed, unwarranted, to claim one is inferring from a purely 'natural' condition to one that is normative. Instead, the natural condition being

My second experiment in being concerns natural evil at a higher level of human functioning, viz. a level we share with most other animals: that of sexuality and reproduction. Imagine a late teenager or young adult, $S_1$, who is sexually violated, not by a stranger or a friend but by their own parent. This is precisely a 'violation' because we assume, and assume rightly, that even if $S_1$ had desired sexual contact with their parent – consciously or unconsciously – and perhaps even derived pleasure from it, such desires and pleasures would be essentially and non-defeasibly disordered. The sexual (unlike our vegetative) powers lie at the core of our personality, so even if they afford pleasure, if they are at the same time abused, we instinctively grasp that an evil has been perpetrated. It follows that consent, in this context, is irrelevant: for even supposing $S_1$ had consented to incestuous sex, and hence rape had not occurred, that would be insufficient to justify it or render it a good. Furthermore, we recognise the manifest natural evil of incest, even if, say, $S_1$'s progeny were cared for. Such eventualities would in no way justify the violations that took place or transform them from natural evils into natural goods. For we recognise that sexual relations between parent and child are an inappropriate form of love: they are, at the very least, a betrayal of the protective function of parenting and effectively privilege short-term gratification over the teleology of a lifetime family relationship.[61]

My third and final experiment in being concerns the most sophisticated level of human functioning, namely rational functioning. Human reason, in its practical aspect, governs how we both sustain our bodies and navigate our lives, while, in its purely intellectual aspect, it distinguishes us absolutely from plant or other animal life. This explains why assaulting (or just neglecting) our minds appears a peculiarly heinous act (or omission), since it affects, deleteriously, *all* our functioning at once. Imagine, then, a person, $S_2$, who is deliberately not taught to read, who is never sent to school or inducted into any institution for the transmission of culture, and who is exposed to only the most rude and crude form of communication. $S_2$ would, after a certain stage, be hampered, irreparably, in their human development and hence suffer from a manifest natural evil of perhaps the most grievous kind; and this judgement does not, it should be

---

elaborated simply *is* normative. (Furthermore, if one purports to infer the evaluative from the purely non-evaluative, what *grounds* – that is, sufficient grounds – could there be for one's inference?) For the ubiquity of value, at least in human life, and how true, full, descriptions of such life are ineluctably evaluative, see Chappell (2017). (I will expand on this point in Section 4.1.)

[61] One piece of evidence for this is the way in which the incest-instigating parent will safeguard their offspring with a view not primarily to the latter's well-being but rather to their own sexual satisfaction. In this way, incest is inseparable from a matrix of intense jealousies, which prevent children from developing a proper relation to their peers (a relation which parents are precisely meant to foster rather than to retard).

noted, await confirmation by some other method. In order to grasp this manifest natural evil as such, we do not need to ask whether, for instance, we could affirm a society in which not just $S_2$ but all human persons were treated in this way. Similarly, we need not ask whether we could agree to a social contract that made such treatment permissible; or whether such treatment is, *per impossibile*, somehow expressive of (or at least compatible with) the virtues. Rather, $S_2$'s treatment is a manifest natural evil precisely because we can tell, immediately, that it is destructive of their functioning – and this at an essential level (human beings being specifically rational animals).

I offer these three experiments in being not as proof but rather as partial corroboration of the *via negativa* bodied forth by Sophocles' *Antigone* and given philosophical heft by Wolff. This method is primarily epistemic, so does not claim to offer systematic or detailed grounds for its judgements – though I have suggested some along the way. Rather, it brings out the anthropological fact that we are most sensitised and receptive to natural law norms 'in the breach', that is, when they are threatened or contravened;[62] and this has significant historical precedent. As Louis Monden remarks, 'Historically the appeal to the natural law has arisen precisely from the resistance of personal conscience to the arbitrariness of written laws; it appeals to an *unwritten law*, [a] . . . knowledge of what man ought to do and ought not to do in order to be and to become authentically himself' (Monden 1966: 89). As Rommen contends, the arbitrariness in question is most egregious when the written law not only departs from but also directly opposes the natural law. As he writes: 'The growth of totalitarian regimes, far from checking or reversing the revival of natural law, has on the contrary contributed mightily to this revival in ever wider circles' (Rommen 1998: 136). And as Yves Simon suggests, this was seen most palpably after World War II. 'Revived interest in the universalism of natural law is partly due', he notes, 'to a reaction against the evil perpetrated during the period of racist predominance' (Simon 1965: 39). Of course, none of the above-discussed experiments in being concern specifically political (let alone totalitarian) breaches of the natural law. Yet each becomes more likely under totalitarian conditions, when States can interfere most readily with people's bodily, familial and intellectual functioning.

Before moving on to investigate two critical challenges to natural law methodology, it is worth highlighting that the sufferings of S, $S_1$ and $S_2$ are

---

[62] Why so? Perhaps we are more sensitive to suffering and misfortune than to flourishing, partly because they make more exigent calls on our agency. There seems also a strong risk of sentimentalism in describing flourishing lives, which is less severe in describing their opposites. This may be one aspect of what Tolstoy intends when he opens *Anna Karenina* with the famous dictum that 'All happy families are alike, but an unhappy family is unhappy after its own fashion' (see Tolstoy 2000).

far from imaginary.[63] They were all visited on the daughter and grandchildren of the Austrian, Josef Fritzl, who imprisoned the former (Elisabeth) in his basement and subsequently repeatedly raped her, producing seven incestuous grandchildren. The latter were, moreover, deprived of an education. The fact that Fritzl had grown up in Nazi Austria may be a coincidence, but equally, it may have contributed to his tyrannical behaviour. Be that as it may, the fact that Fritzl broke the natural law along all three dimensions of being, and each in multiple ways, makes his a particularly horrifying case.[64] When I invoke 'three dimensions of being' here, I am referring, evidently, to that tripartite schema of human functioning elaborated by Aristotle in *NE* 1.7 and later redeployed by Aquinas at *Summa Theologiae* I–II, question 94, article 2. In what follows, then, the central question we should ask is: has any modern critique given us reason to abandon that schema, or to replace it with another? My suggestion is that this Aristotelian-cum-Thomistic template for understanding the normative teleology of life – including, most saliently, human life – has already demonstrated its robustness. As a result, it will take a good deal of theoretical ingenuity and argument to dislodge it. We should be open, nevertheless, to modern theories that attempt to do so, since a lot of philosophy has intervened since the Aristotelian–Thomistic consensus held sway. It is to an exploration and analysis of two such challenges, therefore, that I now turn.

## 4 Two Core Challenges

Although philosophical challenges to the natural law inheritance began in earnest with the scientific revolution of the seventeenth century, they attained their most detailed and rigorous formulation only in the twentieth century, after the development of metaethics and the advent of Darwinian evolutionary biology. The latter, emerging in the late nineteenth century, challenges the very notion of final ends or goal-directedness in nature, maintaining that what appears to be teleological orderedness is merely the product of random mutation and fittedness to particular environments. I want to begin, however, not with this relatively late assault on natural law and its theoretical infrastructure – one that depends essentially on empirical and, more specifically, on various natural scientific developments.[65] Instead, I want to broach matters at the purely philosophical,

---

[63] In this sense, too, they are not just 'thought experiments' – they are (*a fortiori*) experiments in *being*.

[64] For more detail, see Marsh and Pancevski (2009).

[65] Owing to the modern centrality of the 'natural sciences', the very meaning of 'naturalism' has changed. Having encompassed the Aristotelian investigation of nature, it is now typically reduced to the commitments and deliverances of the modern 'hard' sciences (or rather these as mediated by philosophical reflection). This narrowing of sense, though, is question-begging, since it sidelines the original, Aristotelian – and hence both essentialist and teleological – sense

metaethical, level of the 'fact/value distinction'. Although this received its classical formulation in the eighteenth century, in the work of David Hume, it was only in the twentieth century that it found its most sophisticated elaboration, in the work of philosophers like G. E. Moore, C. L. Stevenson, R. M. Hare and J. L. Mackie. While I will focus on Hume, Moore and Mackie, it is worth stressing that the fact/value distinction (or dichotomy) was, for most of the twentieth century – and arguably throughout it – axiomatic within moral philosophy. Granted, and as Christopher Martin contends, its status as an axiom, or, less strictly, as 'conventional wisdom', may well have been confined to anglophone analytic philosophy.[66] Yet given the widespread influence of the latter, together with its admirable standards of precision and rigour, no one can ignore this key, long-standing and multiply ramifying feature of ethical enquiry; and this is so *a fortiori* since, if the fact/value distinction is both well-founded and cogent, the entire tradition of natural law thought becomes severed at its root.

## 4.1 The Fact/Value Distinction

The idea that facts and values, or descriptions and evaluations, form a dichotomous distinction – and hence that there are no evaluative facts about, or true evaluative descriptions of, the world – probably strikes most people (viz. those innocent of philosophical theory) as bizarre.[67] That child abuse or lacking education is bad, for instance, or that having adequate nutrition or exposure to light is good, seem, after all, to be prime candidates for such facts. Nonetheless, and as I have outlined, that the factual and the evaluative are radically disjoint has long been understood among many moral philosophers as something approaching a truism. Why so? There are many reasons, but I want to focus on three central, and widely influential, arguments for this view. First, there is what I will call the metaphysical argument, namely that the world, understood in a substantial sense as what *is* – that is, our ontological surroundings, in all their manifold variety – simply does not, and moreover cannot, contain anything evaluative or normative. Rather, values are somehow projected onto the world, or as Hume puts it,[68] they 'gild' and 'stain' it: they do not, that is, form part of the fabric of the world itself. Second, there is the inferential argument, viz. the claim that no purely non-evaluative proposition (or

---

of *phusis* ('nature', from which we get 'physics'). As I will explore in Section 4.1, G. E. Moore's critique of the so-called naturalistic fallacy is guilty of this reduction.

[66]  See Martin (2004).

[67]  When I refer to the 'world' here, I mean to pick out the natural world, including human activity in all its diverse forms. There are, admittedly, moral realists – e.g. Moorean intuitionists and divine command theorists – who claim there are evaluative facts about the 'world' in some far more etiolated, non-natural (or indeed supernatural) sense, but they are not my concern in what follows.

[68]  See Hume (1998: 89, appendix 1, 21).

set thereof) entails any evaluative proposition. Again originating with Hume, this argument has been referred to often as the 'is/ought' problem, or the claim that no 'ought' follows from a mere 'is'. Third, there is the semantic argument: the core idea being that no evaluative term (typically, the term chosen is 'good') has the same meaning or definition as any 'natural' term (or set thereof). It follows, purportedly, that the natural and the evaluative are completely disjoint. This argument originates with G. E. Moore and his claim, specifically, to have identified the 'naturalistic fallacy'.

Let us begin, then, with the metaphysical argument. This is both the most readily graspable and, arguably, the most striking of the three, since it maintains that value – whether moral or non-moral[69] – is not the kind of property or feature that can inhabit the objective world. As I mentioned, this argument has its origins in Hume, who writes that 'the mind has a great propensity to spread itself on external objects, and to conjoin with them any internal impressions, which they occasion'.[70] When applied to ethics, his claim seems to be that, although value judgements are possible, indeed common, they rest fundamentally not on the intrinsic character of their objects but rather on the reactions such objects elicit. For example, when I judge that child abuse is morally bad, in virtue of the harm done to the child, this judgement – despite its perfectly objective form – comes to rest on no objective 'matters of fact'. All that exist are certain external events – the child undergoing various pains, and so on – and my adverse reaction to them. Granted, my 'internal impression', when confronted with these events, is what we might call 'negative', but this goes no way to establishing that they are *intrinsically* bad. This is, presumably, what Hume intends when, in assessing the moral quality of 'wilful murder', he holds:

> Examine it in all lights, and see if you can find that matter of fact, or real existence, which you call *vice* ... The vice entirely escapes you, as long as you consider the object. You never can find it, till you turn your reflection into your own breast, and find a sentiment of disapprobation ... Here is a matter of fact; but ... It lies in yourself, not in the object.[71]

---

[69] The distinction between the moral and the non-moral is intuitive, but hard to draw precisely. Intuitively, lacking education is bad, so depriving someone of education is morally bad; similarly, nutrition is good, so ensuring someone has enough to eat is morally good. Here the moral involves *choosing* (or failing to choose) base-level, intrinsic goods, which themselves have non-moral – or, better, 'pre-moral' – value ('pre-moral' is John Finnis's term, as I will detail below in Section 5). I deliberately leave out of account non-intrinsic goods, such as the good of flour for the purpose of baking a cake. While one indeed ought to use flour in this context, the 'ought' here is non-moral, since it rests on a purely instrumental, extrinsic good. In what follows, I will concentrate only on intrinsic goods and the moral choices that flow from them.

[70] Hume (2007: 112, 1.3.14.25).    [71] Hume (2007: 301, 3.1.1.26).

This is Hume's most unequivocal anticipation, perhaps, of the fact/value distinction. Even murder is now conceived of as a normatively denuded event or 'object', and its supposed disvalue is reduced to the reaction of those who happen – owing to their contingent constitution or set of dispositions – to disapprove of it.

A superficial criticism of this argument is that, in some of its formulations, it trades on an ambiguity in the notion of 'value'. As Hilary Putnam remarks, whereas 'value' can designate an objective property, in verbal form – as in 'I value him for his wit' – it can mean merely to 'like' or 'enjoy'.[72] Hume's argument, however, goes deeper than this: his contention is that values are always (at best) rooted in mere approvals or disapprovals and never in the intrinsic goods or evils which – prior to the advent of philosophical theory – we take to warrant such attitudes. What are we to make of this? Hume's position not only goes against the surface grammar of most value judgements; it also flies in the face of the value-consciousness of those making such judgements. Perhaps people really are systematically self-deceived about the nature and structure of their value judgements; but it is more likely, I suggest, that the deception lies in Hume's account itself. For it depends on a radically reductive and impoverished conception of what the 'world', or, as he puts it, 'real existence', exhaustively consists in. According to Hume, when we encounter a case of child abuse, say, we encounter a set of inflicted pains, or, even more parsimoniously, a set of C-fibres firing owing to certain stimuli. Some of us react adversely to this, while others, presumably, do not (the abuser, at least, is likely to fall under the latter category). Yet is this a *full and accurate* description of what is going on? Surely not. The C-fibres which undoubtedly fire in this case are more adequately described as suffering, or even torture, and the treatment being meted out is plainly cruel. Yet as soon as we have admitted the greater adequacy of this description, we have admitted a host of values into our ontology, and, moreover, we have conceded that our response or reaction is not merely consequent but also *appropriate* to what is happening. In other words, we have rejected implicitly the highly constrained vision of the world and its contents that Hume has (question-beggingly) tried to enforce.[73]

---

[72] See Putnam (2017: 29, 32).

[73] For a similar argument against Hume, see Oderberg (2000: 14–15). True, when we explicate why the abuser is cruel, or the child suffering, we will appeal to facts that are in some sense more 'basic'. Yet it does not follow that these facts must, by the same token, be evaluatively empty. Rather, in order to remain adequate to the phenomena, they will remain necessarily within what might be called the evaluative 'orbit'. ('He's cruel in that he's ruining the child's sexuality', 'she's suffering because her innocence is being prematurely taken from her', etc.) To insist that such 'thick' evaluative descriptions must give way to something more basic still – namely, a purely non-evaluative mode of description – and that only this level of description is properly objective, is both captious and tendentious. I will revisit the notion that the objective (or what

Hume's metaphysical argument has a twentieth-century counterpart in John Mackie's argument from 'queerness'.[74] This also puts constraints on what the 'world' can contain, but unlike its Humean predecessor, it purports to give principled reasons for doing so. In short, these consist in the claim that any world harbouring objective, intrinsic, values would be 'queer' (i.e. unconscionably odd). As Mackie puts things, if the world did contain value properties of the kind presupposed in ordinary discourse, these would have to be 'qualities or relations of a very strange sort, utterly different from anything else in the universe' (Mackie 1977: 38); and this because such qualities or relations would have to be what he calls 'objective prescriptions': entities guiding our behaviour, or counselling us how to act, which are nonetheless not human beings but entities inscribed, somehow, in the fabric of the universe. With a minimum of reflection, however, and after having scanned the universe for such entities, we can tell these are nowhere to be found. It is not that the existence of such objective values is straightforwardly incoherent or merely self-contradictory – such things could, it appears, exist. It is just that our experience does not contain them, and bar some sophisticated evidence for their existence – comparable, maybe, to microscopic evidence for the existence of bacteria – we simply have no positive reason to affirm them. It is in virtue of this supposed lack of evidence, moreover, that Mackie calls his axiological view an 'error theory': all objective evaluative claims are, he contends, false, since they presuppose entities for which we have no evidence. Further, he rounds off his metaphysical argument with an epistemological coda. Not only (he maintains) would objective, intrinsic, goods and evils entail a queer metaphysics; they would, in turn, entail a queer epistemology. For, in point of fact, we have no faculty or faculties that can discern the kind of 'objective prescriptions' which traditional, objective, value theory – not least natural law theory – requires.

Mackie's error theory is bold and *prima facie* 'tough minded', but, on closer scrutiny, it appears thoroughly simple-minded. It begins by assuming that all genuine existents must be open to empirical observation and verification, and then points out that objective values do not meet these empiricist requirements. They do not show up, as it were, in an inventory of the world's furniture – as itemised by the modern natural sciences. Yet, first of all, to restrict the real to the deliverances of those sciences is tendentious, mirroring Hume's assumption that only a highly parsimonious and impoverished description of the world can

---

truly 'is') must be non-evaluative when I come to the inferential argument. (For the notion of 'thick' concepts, see Kirchin 2013.)

[74] This is an unfortunate term, perhaps, but it has roots in the Anglo-American philosophical milieu of the 1960s. Henry Veatch, for example, refers to 'queer entities' in his 1966 paper, 'Non-Cognitivism in Ethics: A Modest Proposal for its Diagnosis and Cure' (see Veatch 1966: 104).

capture its objective contents. Secondly, this tendentious restriction opens itself to the charge of *tu quoque*, or 'you too!' For surely Mackie wants to admit into his ontology entities that do not conform to his narrow, empiricist, canons of the genuine or *bona fide*. Logical constants, mathematical sets and tautologies are not the kinds of thing we 'bump into' or are discoverable using even the sophisticated methods of the natural sciences. Yet Mackie would not be content merely to write off both logic and mathematics as error theories. There are, moreover, non-logical and non-mathematical notions which, although they do not pick out concrete existents, Mackie would want to retain. Take, for instance, propositions that refer to the future, to boringness, to time, to inertia or to causation. None of these can be straightforwardly pointed to or uncovered by the methods of the natural sciences. Yet Mackie's conversation would end up even more arid than it already is if, in addition to banishing talk involving objective, intrinsic values, he had to jettison these items too. It is hard, therefore, not to agree with Hilary Putnam when he sees not an argument here but rather an expression of 'the last dogma of empiricism', or, as Christopher Martin puts it, 'a profession of materialist and empiricist faith'.[75]

The second, inferential, argument for the fact/value distinction also derives from Hume. Here the focus is not on the metaphysically (supposedly) *outré* nature of values but on the logically unbridgeable gap that holds (allegedly) between purely non-evaluative propositions and their evaluative counterparts. As Hume maintains:

> In every system of morality, which I have hitherto met with, I have always remarked, that the author ... makes observations concerning human affairs; when of a sudden I am surprised to find, that instead of the usual copulations of propositions, *is*, and *is not*, I meet with no proposition that is not connected with an *ought*, or an *ought not*.

Further, he adds that he thinks it 'altogether inconceivable, how this new relation can be a deduction from others, which are entirely different from it'.[76] Now, first off, it should be acknowledged that the way Hume expresses his argument is

---

[75] See Putnam (2002: 145) and Martin (2004: 59), respectively. Cf. Putnam on Mackie as a 'reductive materialist' (Putnam 2017: 34), whose argument from queerness wipes away not only moral but also epistemic values like coherence and economy (Putnam 2002: 142; cf. Cuneo 2007, esp. chs 3–4). (For a similar critique of Mackie's argument, albeit formulated against Hume, see Oderberg 2000: 10–11.) It is worth noting, in addition, that Mackie's specification of objective, intrinsic, values as 'objective prescriptions' is markedly tendentious. Objective goods and evils are not themselves prescriptions, even if people rightly prescribe on their basis. As Aquinas holds, 'the good is to be done and pursued, and evil to be avoided' ('bonum est faciendum et prosequendum, et malum vitandum'; *Summa Theologiae* I–II, 94.2). To assent to and act on this axiom is not, *pace* Mackie, to embrace a 'queer' ontology of objective prescriptions. It is merely to respond, as a moral agent, to how the world is.

[76] See Hume (2007: 302, 3.1.1).

misleading. For, if we take him at his word, his view would be that no proposition(s) containing the verb 'to be' – *qua* copula, that is – entail(s) any proposition containing the verb 'ought'; and this is false, since if we combine the copula with clearly evaluative predicates – for example, 'is good', 'is morally execrable' – then an 'ought'-type conclusion follows unproblematically.[77] Given this, I suggest (along with most interpreters) that Hume's intention in invoking 'is'-type propositions is not to pick out any declarative use of the copula but rather to identify those propositions expressing what he calls 'matters of fact', that is, uncontroversially non-evaluative states of affairs. It is such claims, he holds, which do not entail – taken either singly or jointly – any evaluative ('ought') claim(s); and if so, we have a problem. For now, values, besides being metaphysically homeless (by Hume's lights), have been logically severed, too, from any grounding in the objective world. Once again, therefore, they find themselves without a foothold in the 'natural', rendering them – at least from the point of view of the natural law tradition – doubly illegitimate.[78]

Hume's inferential argument has inspired many attempts at refutation. One notable attempt is made by John Searle.[79] Searle claims that one can derive evaluative conclusions from purely non-evaluative premises, the vehicle for doing so being what he dubs 'institutional' as opposed to 'brute' facts (Searle 1964: 55).[80] While the latter are governed by 'regulative rules', which regulate antecedently and independently existing things and practices, the former are governed by 'constitutive rules', which not only regulate – but also create – the practices they govern. Searle's main example of an institutional fact is promising: for while rule-governed, the practice of promising is also brought into being by the rules that regulate it. Crucially, he contends that institutional facts – when embedded in propositions, and without any evaluative supplementation – entail evaluative conclusions. Drawing on his central example, it follows that once S makes a promise, S ought to obey it. Searle lays out his argument in five steps:

---

[77] E.g. 'rape is morally execrable, therefore one ought not to commit it'. In other examples, it would be more plausible to add a *ceteris paribus* clause ('. . . other things being equal'). Yet, even here, we have a logically robust connection between 'is' and 'ought' – notwithstanding the existence of certain defeating conditions. The Humean is likely to object that even premises containing 'good' (or 'bad') do not entail an 'ought'-type conclusion: the latter requires a further premiss to the effect that one ought to do the good (or avoid the bad). The natural lawyer can respond, in turn, that such additional premises merely make explicit the first principle of practical reason (cf. Note 23) – which natural law theory simply takes for granted. Yet the dialectic here is anyway idle. For the vital point – which I elaborate further three paragraphs below – is that natural law arguments never trade in premises that (as I put things in Note 73) wholly prescind from the evaluative 'orbit'.

[78] Hume no doubt welcomed and, indeed, sought this de-legitimation, since his philosophical agenda (like that of Hobbes) is aimed centrally at the repudiation of the Aristotelian inheritance.

[79] See 'How to Derive "Ought" from "Is"' (Searle 1964).

[80] Searle appears to use 'fact' to mean 'state of affairs' rather than 'true proposition'.

(1) Jones uttered the words 'I hereby promise to pay you, Smith, five dollars'; (2) Jones promised to pay Smith five dollars; (3) Jones placed himself under (undertook) an obligation to pay Smith five dollars; (4) Jones is under an obligation to pay Smith five dollars; (5) Jones ought to pay Smith five dollars (see Searle 1964: 44). Searle's fundamental contention is that, while (5) is an evaluative conclusion, at no point are the premisses that support it themselves evaluative, or in need of evaluative supplementation (i.e. the argument is not enthymematic). Furthermore, he suggests that the argument does not merely unfold a tautology, to the effect that promises (necessarily and by definition) ought to be kept. Far from it: the conclusion is informative and, given the truth of the premisses, adds to, rather than merely reiterates, what we already knew.

It is tempting to see Searle's argument as facing a destructive dilemma. *Either* it does require an additional evaluative premiss or premisses, in order to solidify the 'to be doneness' or gerundive force of promising (for why keep a promise – or fulfil an obligation – if these are not *good* things to do?) *or* the argument indeed collapses into a tautology, in which case all it achieves is an explication of the notion of promising, rather than adding anything substantive to our knowledge of the practice. Both for the sake of argument and of charity, however, I think we should accept Searle's claim that his argument is neither enthymematic nor – since it does seem genuinely informative – reducible to a tautology. Rather, we should focus our criticism on his structuring conception of 'institutional facts'. Searle's view is that making a promise imports an obligation and enjoins a moral (or as he puts it, 'categorical') 'ought', in virtue of the institution of promising. The promiser is bound, that is, to keep his promises, on pain of misconstruing and, in effect, overturning the practice of which he is a part. Yet is this 'boundness' properly moral in kind, rather than merely an *expectation* attendant upon a particular type of practice? For if the 'oughtness' here were genuinely moral, any institution would, simply in virtue of being extant, yield moral entailments. An inquisitor, for instance, having pronounced an individual a 'heretic', would, simply in virtue of having followed the protocols of the Inquisition, be under an obligation – and hence 'ought' – to punish the heretic (even to death); but far from corroborating Searle's deployment of the idea of 'institutional facts', this seems a *reductio* of it. Likewise, in the (comparatively innocuous) case of, say, being a fireman, one can conclude that fireman Sam is, in virtue of occupying his role, expected to put out fires. It is another thing altogether, though, to conclude that he *ought* to do so. This would follow if and only if the institution of firefighting can be shown, independently, to be a morally good institution.[81]

---

[81] Searle objects that this conception of institutions takes an essentially 'external' view of them, one mirrored in Proudhon's view of property as 'theft' (see Searle 1964: 57 n. 8). He then adjures that this external approach to institutions can't be taken across the board, since there are practices we

All in all, then, and despite the ingeniousness of Searle's argument, I suggest that Hume's inferential argument remains standing. Yet, if so, does it matter? Would Hume's triumph be injurious to traditional natural law reasoning, cutting it off from any grounding in nature? Thinkers like John Finnis, a proponent of the 'new' natural law theory, believe so, and hence – as we shall see in Section 5 – they attempt to rid natural law of any direct or significant dependence on nature. This strategy, however, is unwarranted. For, as I have already suggested, in actual contexts of natural law debate, we never have to 'get behind' the evaluative phenomena to something more basic and (supposedly) more objective. No doubt there are purely non-evaluative descriptions that could be offered of the phenomena in question: descriptions solely in terms of atoms, molecules, chemical interactions and so on. Yet this level of description is simply irrelevant to grasping and reasoning about the events with which and persons with whom we are concerned. If we are interested in *these*, any descriptions of them will be already and inevitably couched in evaluative terms – terms that are, moreover, perfectly objective, given the ontological domain over which we are quantifying (we are not doing organic chemistry, after all). Crucially, therefore, since our most basic terms of description here are inflected, necessarily, with value, we will have no problem inferring evaluative conclusions from them. Hume's inferential argument will, in other words – even if cogent – have no bite, since its hyper-parsimonious conception of the 'objective' is never encountered in the context of natural law argumentation. We can, in short, happily accept his argument but at the same time roundly deny that it undermines the kind of inferences natural lawyers seek to draw.[82]

The third argument for the fact/value distinction is semantic in kind. It is given classical expression in G. E. Moore's *Principia Ethica* (Moore 1903) and takes aim at the idea that 'goodness' – understood as the paradigm and most general value concept – admits of a naturalistic definition. What Moore intends by 'naturalistic' is any meaning-complex that rests on the deliverances of the

---

form part of willy-nilly. Perhaps so. It seems reasonable to say that if, for example, one affirms p along with p > q, one ought to affirm q. Yet the 'ought' in question here, for all its inevitability, is not moral in kind. I would challenge Searle to find any institutional facts that, in and of themselves, have moral sequelae.

[82] E.g. 'child abuse is cruel and severely debilitates a child's sexuality; therefore, one ought not to commit child abuse'. It is worth highlighting that the costs of adhering to Hume's narrow conception of the 'objective' (*qua* purely non-evaluative) are profound. They involve explaining how the evaluative supervenes on the non-evaluative, even though the barrenness of the latter terrain precludes any evaluative foothold. For a collection aimed at explicating such purported supervenience, see *Ethical Naturalism* (Nuccetelli and Seay 2012). Notably, all the contributors to this volume construe 'nature' in Humean, rather than Aristotelian, terms. This makes the problem of supervenience intractable, yet none of the authors questions their obstructive – and highly counterproductive – theoretical construal.

modern natural sciences.[83] A key example here would be pleasure, the preferred conception of the good among classical utilitarians. Moore hopes to show, in short, that goodness cannot consist in pleasure – or any other naturalistic property or set of properties – in virtue of two tests: the first being purely semantic, while the second is semantic-cum-epistemic. The first test runs as follows. Let us assume that goodness reduces to, say, pleasure. It follows that we can define 'goodness' as 'the pleasant'; and, if so, we are judging that these two concepts are identical in meaning. Yet it follows from this, in turn, that 'the good is the pleasant' is merely tautologous. For, given that goodness reduces to pleasure, we are claiming, uninformatively, that the pleasant is the pleasant. This upshot is semantically untoward, however: for to claim that 'goodness' means 'the pleasant' certainly sounds informative. So we can conclude that our naturalistic definition of 'goodness' as 'pleasure' must be false, since in asserting it we are asserting more than a mere tautology. The second test is related, but distinct, and is usually called the 'open question argument'.[84] Here Moore argues that, if goodness were definable as, say, the greatest happiness of the greatest number, its meaning would be 'closed'. That is, it would not be possible to ask, with significance, whether goodness is, in fact, thus naturistically defined. Yet we can tell that – far from being settled – it is perfectly possible to raise such a question: as Moore puts it, the question remains 'open'. He concludes that we have failed (once more) to define 'goodness': indeed, any naturalistic definition of 'good' or its cognates remains interminably 'open'.

In sum, Moore holds that any attempt to give 'goodness' a naturalistic definition commits what he calls the 'naturalistic fallacy'; but must any definition of goodness in naturalistic terms – on which natural law theory also depends[85] – be ill-founded? No. As to the first test, we can impugn Moore's assumption that merely because two terms pick out the same metaphysical property, they are, by the same token, identical in *meaning*. Even in cases of analytic definition – for instance, where 'triangle' is the *definiendum* and 'three-sided figure whose angles add up to 180 degrees' is the *definiens* – we have some semantic gain. Moreover, if so, our semantic grasp increases *a fortiori* when the *definiendum* has naturalistic content. For to discover that, for example, 'goodness' means 'the pleasant' is to learn something significant. It is significant, indeed, even though (*ex hypothesi*) goodness and pleasure are identical

---

[83] See Moore (1903: 38–41).    [84] See Moore (1903: 11–17).

[85] Provided, that is, that 'naturalistic' is interpreted in an Aristotelian sense, i.e. in a more capacious way than Moore (in this respect, following Hume) allows. In line with this, we can define 'goodness' as the actualisation of a substance's potentiality, or as the realisation of its essential powers.

properties and have been so all along.[86] As to the second test, Moore rests a lot of weight on the so-called open feel of any naturalistic definition of 'goodness'. One response to this would be to hold that such openness is relative to speakers: for the hedonist, for instance, defining 'goodness' as 'the pleasant' is settled or closed.[87] Yet this is very unpromising, since it makes semantic openness and closedness psychologically incorrigible, that is, a matter of first-person author-ity and hence immune to objective challenge. A more promising response would be to question the salience of whether a proposed definition feels open or closed in the first place. After all, defining 'goodness' is a rarefied and philosophically complex endeavour, and any well-worked-out proposal is likely to be open to dispute in some respect(s). So it stands to reason that any serious definition will not feel *completely* settled or closed. Moore's misstep here is to infer that, in virtue of this, no such definition can be true. Granted, any challenges to the proposed definition should be addressed and, where these are rationally weighty, it should be adjusted; but some people will, unfortu-nately, remain unpersuaded, their refusal to assent to the *definiens* being, simply, a recalcitrance to the truth.

If this line of criticism sounds dismissive of rational objection, it can be fortified as follows. Moore reasons that, since no naturalistic definition of 'goodness' is closed – that is, for any such definition, there are those who dispute it, in whole or in part – all such definitions are open; and if they remain open, then the definition of 'goodness' cannot be of a naturalistic type. Yet this presupposes that openness and closedness are related as contradictories: if, that is, definition D is not open, it must be closed, while if D is not closed, it must be open. My suggestion, however, is that the openness and closedness of a definition are related not as contradictories but as contraries. In other words, even if a definition is not closed, it does not follow that it is open, because there is a third possibility, namely that it is neither open nor closed but of such a kind that the test of openness and closedness is inapplicable and, indeed, irrelevant. For, once again, there may be domains of enquiry that are sufficiently difficult, and hence obscure to the intelligence, that neither openness nor closedness in definition is pertinent to deciding their truth. My claim is that the definition of 'goodness' is of this sort. True, the natural law definition of 'goodness' as – to put matters succinctly – the actualisation of a substance's potentiality, or,

---

[86] Moore's conflation between meanings and metaphysical properties is criticised in Frankena (1939). Frankena's criticism is anticipated by Aquinas, who notes that, even though goodness and perfected being are the same metaphysically, they are not the same semantically. As he puts matters, in scholastic idiom: 'Although goodness and [perfected or actualised] being are the same really, nevertheless since they differ in thought, they are not predicated of a thing absolutely in the same way' (*Summa Theologiae* I, 5.1 response).

[87] William Frankena adopts this line (see Frankena 1939).

alternatively, as the realisation of a thing's essential powers, is hardly settled on first inspection and requires much investigation even to be rendered plausible. Yet this is exactly what one should expect in such an abstract and abstruse area of enquiry. Once one has done the investigative legwork, and countenanced other both naturalistic and non-naturalistic definitions, one will come to be persuaded of this naturalistic definition's rational merits. Not that this is tantamount to the natural law definition of 'goodness' being closed, any more than definitions of space and time are. Yet such settledness is, in the final analysis, an unreasonable and unwarranted expectation and should not be our aim.[88]

## 4.2 Evolutionary Biology

I have argued, then, that the foregoing metaethical threats to natural law theory – namely, the metaphysical, inferential and semantic arguments – are defeasible and hence (at least *pro tanto*) leave that theory intact. Another threat immediately looms, however, this time from an empirical and, more specifically, natural scientific direction. This threat originated with the work on 'evolution' by Jean-Baptiste Lamarck and Herbert Spencer, this gaining key support from Charles Darwin, whose detailed biological investigations suggested that natural, living species – including, most notably, the human species – had evolved through a process he called 'natural selection'.[89] When combined with subsequent corroborative and ampliative research in the twentieth century, evolutionary biology imperils two key tenets of Aristotelian naturalism and thereby traditional natural law theory. First, it denies the eternality and fixity (or unchangingness) of biological species, affirming, instead, that they develop over time and give rise to new species that survive in virtue of being 'fitter' than their competitors.[90] In this way, it seems radically to impugn the traditional natural law view that biological species – most saliently, the human species – have an *essence*, which does not change and that is clearly distinct from other species essences. Secondly, evolutionary biology appears wholly inhospitable to the idea that biological species are intrinsically ordered to certain correlative *ends*,

---

[88] For treatments of the open question argument along similar, though not the same, lines, see Veatch (1966: 105–8); Simpson (2001: 110–13); Oderberg (2020: 19–21). It is worth pointing out that Moore's own positive characterisation of 'goodness' as a simple, non-natural and indefinable(!) quality, akin to a colour property like yellow, hardly passes the open question test (it remains eminently 'open'). Then again, if my argument is cogent, this *per se* is not a point against it: its weaknesses lie elsewhere. If the reader is interested in exploring these, I suggest the three sources cited in this note.

[89] For an excellent introduction to evolution and natural selection, which is sensitive to the concerns of natural lawyers, see Gilson (1984).

[90] For Darwin's notion of fitness as indexed to reproductive power, see Lewens (2007: 46). Subsequent conceptions of fitness have highlighted its relativity to particular environments, thereby distancing it from specifically reproductive fitness.

or as R. B. Braithwaite puts it, demonstrate teleological 'direction' without a 'director'.[91] Rather, it holds that – even if organisms appear to be end-directed – this is merely the result of random mutations, which happen to lend them greater 'survival value' in particular environments. Yet this concatenation of happenstance is insufficient to warrant the traditional natural law idea that species are intrinsically directed to specific ends or goods.

This combined assault on essences-with-ends is thus an attack on both *essentialism* and natural *teleology* – that is, the metaphysical hallmarks, as I have maintained, of natural law theory. Furthermore, many philosophers assume the success of this attack. As to the idea of natural essences, W. K. C. Guthrie holds that 'Doubtless this is not a satisfactory explanation of reality. For one thing it makes Darwinian evolution impossible' (Guthrie 1981: 222; cf. Okasha 2002: 191). Elliott Sober claims that 'Essentialism about species is today a dead issue' (Sober 1992: 249), while Paul Griffiths writes that 'Folk essentialism is both false and fundamentally inconsistent with the Darwinian view of species' (Griffiths 2002: 72). Alex Rosenberg contends that 'The proponents of contemporary species definitions are all agreed that species have no essence' (Rosenberg 1985: 203), while John Dupré avers that 'it is widely recognized that Darwin's theory of evolution rendered untenable the classical essentialist conception of species' (Dupré 1999: 3). As to natural teleology, Oderberg refers to the 'almost pathological distaste' for Aristotelian teleology in Hobbes and his followers (Oderberg 2008: 259). And Bernard Williams asserts, with characteristic aplomb, that the 'first and hardest lesson of Darwinism' is that there is simply no teleology in nature (Williams 1995: 109–10). Notwithstanding this conventional wisdom, in what follows I will argue that neither essentialism nor natural teleology is dead. Indeed, we can allow that living species are non-eternal,[92] change over time, emerge from one another and sometimes go extinct, without giving up the notion of species essences. Moreover, we can allow that species evolve through 'natural selection' without thereby discarding the idea of species goods, to which species members are intrinsically directed. The appearance of incompatibility here is ill-founded, and, despite the broad consensus to which it has

---

[91] See Braithwaite (1946: i). In the nineteenth century, the 'director' in question was assumed to be the transcendent God of Western tradition; but the Aristotelian view is that what directs species to their end (*telos*) or ends is, primarily, an immanent form or *eidos* (each essence (*ousia*) being correlated with a specific form). For how this immanentist view was displaced in the early modern period, see Feser (2015).

[92] 'Species' here, and from now on, refers to the 'infima' or lowest natural species falling under a natural genus. This is how the term is normally used in biology and stands in contrast to 'species' in the pure, philosophical, sense of 'kind'.

given rise, it is one that is increasingly (and with good reason) itself under threat.[93]

To begin, then, I want to tackle the foundational notion of species. Natural law theorists are committed, first, to the reality of species, for, without this basic assumption – that species 'cut nature at its joints' and do not constitute a mere projection or useful fiction – the claims they make about human nature would be baseless. In general, the post-Darwinian consensus supports this realism, even though there are philosophers of biology who make some concessions to nominalism about species.[94] Secondly, natural law theorists are committed to what Michael Devitt calls 'intrinsic biological essentialism' (Devitt 2008: 378), that is, the view that species have essential features or properties that are intrinsic to them. This underwrites the Aristotelian view that, for instance, humans are essentially animals – this being their genus – and animals of an essentially rational kind (this being their 'differentia'). Their animality and rationality are, moreover, not a function of anything extrinsic or relational, even if certain extrinsic relations must obtain in order for human rationality to develop fully. In this respect, there is a clear tension between intrinsic biological essentialism and the now dominant conception of species, namely the 'pheno-typical-cladistic' concept.[95] This holds that species are defined by their members' ability to interbreed, a capacity that is reflected, in turn, by their inhabiting a particular lineage or 'clade'.[96] Richard Boyd refers to this as the 'genea-logical' conception of species, which rests not on organisms' intrinsic features but rather on their relation to other organisms with whom they share a common ancestor (Boyd 1999: 210; cf. Lewens 2007: 74–5, 80). This 'biological species concept' hence founds what Boyd calls 'relational essentialism', a view that – though it purports to be a form of species essentialism – is irrevocably (and indeed consciously) removed from that of traditional natural law theory.

Is this a problem for natural lawyers? It would be, if they had no arguments against the extrinsicist, relational, conception of species posited by cladism; but they are not bereft of counterarguments. For, if we ask what renders a particular organism O a member of species S, the cladist will have recourse to O's

---

[93] I should add that I will be addressing evolutionary biology as a threat only to natural law theory, not as a general threat to any form of moral realism. For those interested in the latter topic, see 'Evolutionary Debunking of Moral Realism' (Vavova 2015).

[94] E.g. Dupré, who speaks of the 'eurocentrism' of actual species categories, yet also the need for scientists to respect this 'folk' classification (at least to some extent – see Dupré 1999: 16–18). See also Lewens (2007: 72–5) on how Darwin's flirtation with nominalism about species settled into a 'general realism'.

[95] Oderberg counts twenty-two definitions of species in the literature (see Oderberg 2007: 209; cf. Devitt 2008: 356).

[96] This conception became dominant largely through the work of Willi Hennig (see Oderberg 2007: 214). For a precise definition of cladism, see Oderberg (2007: 220).

ancestry: ultimately, to the ancestor A which initiated the clade of which O forms a part. Yet what makes A itself a member of S? Here the cladist will have either to point to or postulate A's ancestry, thereby initiating a regress,[97] or to pick out a 'paradigm' ancestor P and claim that O's species membership is defined by O's genealogical relation to P. Yet neither strategy is properly explanatory – we are still left wondering what essential properties O, A and P *share* that make them all members of S. To be told that they each share a lineage is merely to restate what itself stands in need of explanation; and this suggests that the 'relational essentialism' which Boyd invokes is, in point of fact, not a genuine essentialism at all: its reliance on extrinsic relations to other organisms simply relocates the explanatory burden, without discharging it.[98] At best, what cladism offers are necessary properties of a species, which flow from its essence, namely that it can breed with others of its kind and thereby continue a lineage; but this identification of what the scholastics call a species' *propria* is not yet to determine its essence. Indeed, properly understood, it is merely to identify certain diachronic, genealogical, data which themselves can be explained only by synchronic, intrinsic, features of the organisms involved. That is, it is O's species essence that explains with whom it can breed and share a genealogy, not vice versa.[99] Yet, once this is admitted, the cladist must admit, in turn, that he has offered the natural lawyer nothing approaching what is explanatorily needed, viz. an account of intrinsic species essence.

At this point in the dialectic between the evolutionary biologist and natural lawyer, a threefold plan of attack suggests itself – each prong of which is meant to undermine the very notion that species have intrinsic essences. First, evolutionary biology holds that species are not eternal: they come into being through variation and mutation and go extinct when 'selected against' by competition with other species and/or by inclement environmental conditions.[100] Yet this, it is claimed, goes against the traditional Aristotelian notion that species – along

---

[97] Cf. Oderberg (2007: 218); Devitt (2008: 357, 361). An analogy here is the Nazi regime's attempt to define who counted as Jewish. The definition given was in terms of how many Jewish grandparents an individual had. Yet to the question, 'what makes a grandparent Jewish?', the same, fundamentally uninformative – because extrinsicist and relational – answer was given. A properly essentialist answer was never arrived at.

[98] Cf. Oderberg (2007: 216, 222); Devitt (2008: 352, 363); Feser (2019b: 402). Worse, the appeal to extrinsic relations here assimilates natural, living, species to artefacts, which have no internal principle of operation and depend wholly on external agency for their constitution (see Oderberg 2007: 223; Feser 2015: 41, 43; Feser 2019b: 434). This creates an embarrassing affinity with Darwin's opponents, who tended to understand organisms precisely and exhaustively as artefacts of an external agent, viz. God.

[99] Cf. Oderberg (2007: 238, 240); Devitt (2008: 367, 369).

[100] For the role of variation in creating new species out of old, see Lewens (2007: 70) and Devitt (2008: 370).

with their essences – are eternal. Secondly, evolutionary biology maintains that, within the life of a species, there is marked change and development. According to Boyd, for instance, species are nothing over and above 'homeostatic property clusters' (HPCs), and these constituent properties come and go over time.[101] According to Devitt, species consist in 'clusters of covarying chromosomal and genetic traits', while, for Lewens, they amount to 'diagnostic sets' of features that evince a merely 'piecemeal resemblance'.[102] Yet, if so, then the traditional Aristotelian commitment to 'fixed', unchanging, essences is unresponsive to the empirical evidence and must be abandoned. Thirdly, evolutionary biology contends that, in virtue of species variability, and the concomitant fact that new species emerge from old, there are (at best) only vague species boundaries. This has led philosophers of science like Brian Ellis to eschew biological essences altogether, claiming they are too 'messy', unlike the supposedly clean essences that populate chemistry and physics.[103] Further, Kevin de Queiroz holds that 'everything we know about species tells us that they are inherently difficult to circumscribe, particularly in the early stages of divergence; that they are not always sharply distinct, easily recognized entities; and that unambiguous assignment of all organisms to species taxa will be difficult, if not impossible'.[104] Again, the lesson seems to be that the intrinsic biological essentialism affirmed by traditional natural law is outmoded and unworkable.

These three prongs of attack are, however, far from probative. To begin with, the non-eternality of species has been accepted by natural lawyers ever since their embrace of monotheism, which assumes a created, non-eternal world. Evolution through natural selection merely adds another ground for such non-eternality.[105] Any residual concerns about eternality therefore lie elsewhere and most likely depend on a conflation between species and species essences. For the fact that a species – for instance, the dodo – goes extinct does not entail that its essence does.[106] The latter has atemporal content and fails simply to be *instantiated* when the last dodo dies. As to the claim that species vary over time, and thus cannot embody a genuine essence, this verges on metaphysical solecism. Granted, a species' accidental features can come and go, but if it displays no persistent non-accidental features, then in what sense is it identifiable as a species in the first place? Those who gesture in this argumentative direction seem, as Devitt maintains, to be strongly exaggerating or else misinterpreting

---

[101]  See Boyd (1999: 141–2, 167).

[102]  See, respectively, Devitt (2008: 371) (who is following Okasha 2002: 197) and Lewens (2007: 90–1).

[103]  See Ellis (2001).     [104]  See de Queiroz (1999: 79–80).

[105]  See (e.g.) O'Rourke (2004: 46–7) and Feser (2019b: 426–30).

[106]  Cf. Oderberg (2007: 204) and Feser (2019b: 401).

the empirical evidence.[107] Something similar could be said of those who infer from the gradual evolution of species, and hence the existence of intermediary taxa, to the indeterminacy of species. It is perfectly intelligible to claim that – given the state of the empirical evidence and our inexact terms of description – widespread *epistemic* indeterminacy still infects our grasp of different species and their interrelations.[108] Yet to hold that evolutionary biology mandates the *ontological* indeterminacy of species seems, once again, a metaphysical bridge too far.[109] For not only are there many species that are manifestly and incontrovertibly distinct but to allow ontological indeterminacy in any area of enquiry is to court multiple metaphysical conundra, not least (in this domain) the notion that one species is also another or that one organism has two natures.[110]

So the natural law view of species essence is not only coherent; it has proved both empirically and metaphysically robust. The dominant phenotypical-cladistic definition of species is inadequate and is better understood as a designation of species' *propria* than the uncovering of their essence.[111] Furthermore, the non-eternality, changingness and dynamic fissiparousness of individual species cannot be predicated of their respective essences: indeed, to allow this would be to fall into metaphysical incoherence; and, if so, then we have insulated the crucial notion of species essence from three key prongs of attack. None of this addresses, however, let alone upholds, the second vital element of intrinsic biological essentialism, as understood by traditional natural law theory, namely that species essences are intrinsically directed or ordered to particular, correlative ends. In other words, we still need to defend natural law teleology. It is to this task that I now turn.

---

[107] See Devitt (2008: 371) (cf. Oderberg 2007: 212). As examples of such exaggeration, take the following: 'no genotypic characteristic can be postulated as a species essence; the genetic variability found in sexual populations is prodigious' (Sober 1992: 272); 'Intra-specific genetic variation is extremely wide – meiosis, genetic recombination and random mutation together ensure an almost unlimited variety in the range of possible genotypes that the members of a sexually reproducing species can exemplify' (Okasha 2002: 196). Yet even Okasha admits that 'there are important genetic similarities between members of a single species' (Okasha 2002: 197), and Ernst Mayr – who also repudiates intrinsic biological essentialism – refers to 'the historically evolved genetic program shared by all members of the species' (Mayr 1992: 17).

[108] Cf. Oderberg (2007: 229, 234); Devitt (2008: 349, 373–5); Feser (2019b: 405).

[109] Cf. Oderberg (2007: 226); Feser (2019a: 294).

[110] As to what a species essence consists in at the empirical level, Mayr's implied view is, as was seen in Note 107, that it consists in a 'genetic program' (Mayr 1992: 17), something echoed in Devitt's reference to the genome (Devitt 2008: 351). Fran O'Rourke, for his part, speculates that an organism's species essence lies in its DNA (O'Rourke 2004: 11–12, 45) and is evidenced by the latter's entelechy (pp. 52–5).

[111] For the distinction between x's essence and x's necessary properties, see Oderberg (2007: 212, 229).

Many, if not most, current philosophers take it as axiomatic that evolution by natural selection constitutes 'the revenge of Empedocles' (Solinas 2015: 11).[112] That is, they assume that the evolutionary process is wholly 'blind' or directionless and, as such, precludes any 'final' or end-directed explanations. At the global level, this is evident, supposedly, in natural selection's dependence on random genetic mutation, which renders such 'selection' a mere anthropocentric metaphor.[113] At the local level, meanwhile, what may appear as finality within individual functions – for example, the heart's 'purpose' of pumping blood – can be explained in purely material and 'efficient' terms.[114] These global and local forms of explanatory reduction are targeted not just at the idea of natural ends but also, crucially, at any telic normativity. In other words, nature is to be evacuated of ends also *qua* goods, as philosophers like Mark Bedau, John Hawthorne and Daniel Nolan all agree.[115] Such philosophers may grant some residual room for value in the case of 'minded' creatures, for human action is mediated by choice, and hence occurs (at least usually) under the 'guise of the good'.[116] Yet, even here, such value is likely to be reduced to mere subjective desire, since it does not reflect any goods that are sponsored by nature or natural processes; and this underlines the fact that, on this 'Empedoclean', strongly reductionist view, any firmly teleological explanations must be illegitimate. At most, such explanations are a purveyor of 'intellectual satisfaction' (Braithwaite 1946: vii), appealing, perhaps, to our familiarity with artefacts and the way we impose both ends and values on them (cf. Lewens 2004); but this is mere 'as if' finalism, as several authors put it.[117] *Per se* and intrinsically, no species is a proper locus of teleological explanation, at either a global or a local level. There are, in sum, no ends or goods in nature.

This view of the deliverances of evolutionary biology is, however, open to challenge. At a global level, Darwin himself speaks in teleological terms. 'Natural selection', he writes, 'is daily and hourly scrutinising ... every variation, even the slightest; rejecting that which is bad, preserving and adding up all that is good; silently and insensibly working ... at the improvement of each organic being' (Darwin 1996: 70). This both telic and value-laden conception of

---

[112] Empedocles was a pre-Socratic philosopher who anticipated the idea of evolution through natural selection. Unlike Darwin, however, he seems not to have investigated his hypothesis at an empirical level.

[113] Cf. Gilson (1984: 75–6) and Feser (2019b: 412–13).

[114] See (e.g.) Bedau (1992: 795). 'Material', 'efficient' and 'final' are, of course, Aristotelian terms of art. 'Formal' explanation aligns with final and is equally precluded by evolutionary biology – at least according to the broad philosophical consensus I am outlining.

[115] See Bedau (1992: 803–4) and Hawthorne and Nolan (2006: 281), respectively.

[116] See (e.g.) Bedau (1992: 801–2) and Hawthorne and Nolan (2006: 282).

[117] See (e.g.) Gilson (1984: 76); Bedau (1992: 783) on C. D. Broad; Lewens (2004: 166); O'Rourke (2004: 29 n. 86, 32) on Ghiselin.

evolution is upheld also by Darwin's followers: Asa Gray, for example, holds that 'We recognize the great service rendered by Darwin to natural science by restoring teleology to it';[118] and this conception of evolution as having an overall, normative, direction is not confined to nineteenth-century thinkers. Evolution's 'magnification' of better adapted forms (Lewens 2007: 60–1) has been dubbed 'creative' by the evolutionary biologist and philosopher Francisco Ayala, and several philosophers of biology – notably David Depew – have followed suit.[119] Such natural 'creativity' presupposes not extrinsic, let alone divine action, but rather that the 'chance' or 'random' mutations spoken of by evolutionary biologists demonstrate an intrinsic potentiality for better adapted, 'fitter' organic forms.[120] This view thus brings evolutionary development far closer to Aristotle than to Empedocles. For, as Aristotle maintains, 'Absence of chance and conduciveness to ends are to be found in the works of Nature especially, and the end of her generations and combinations is a form of the beautiful [*kalon*]' (*Parts of Animals* 644b–5a). Notwithstanding his use of the emotive value-term 'beautiful', one can appreciate the deep affinity between Aristotle's view here and the teleological understanding of evolution I have outlined. Further, if philosophers as different as Etienne Gilson and Thomas Nagel have come to share this understanding, it cannot be dismissed as simply disreputable or unworthy of philosophical consideration.[121]

Now if natural law theory highlights the goods of health, reproduction and knowledge, and these are conducive to species fitness and survival, there

---

[118] Quoted in Gilson (1984: 84). Darwin replies that 'What you say about teleology pleases me especially'. Both Francis Darwin and Thomas Huxley agree with Gray (see Gilson 1984: 84–5). For more on Darwin's teleological language, see Lewens (2004: 29–30); Lewens (2007: 41, 51–3); Feser (2019b: 390, 419).

[119] See Ayala (1970) and Depew (2008), respectively. For more on evolution as demonstrating 'creativity' in the promotion of new, 'fitter' organisms, see Gilson (1984: 87); Lewens (2004: 31–2; 2007: 53).

[120] For the idea that mutations presuppose an intrinsic potentiality for change, see Gilson (1984: 51–2); O'Rourke (2004: 34, 41); Feser (2019b: 425, 431). Assuming this potentiality rests on 'dormant' or 'cryptic' genes, it is possible that mutations are not properly 'chance' events at all but rather bear witness to determinate – yet admittedly obscure or ill-understood – causation (Lewens 2007: 44). O'Rourke goes so far as to call these 'directed mutations' (O'Rourke 2004: 52). Indeed, according to James Lennox, 'Selection explanations are inherently teleological, in the sense that a value consequence (Darwin most often uses the term "advantage") of a trait explains its increase, or presence, in a population … Darwin essentially re-invented teleology … The concept of selection permits the extension of the teleology of domestic breeding into the natural domain, without the need of conscious design' (Lennox 1993: 410, 417).

[121] Gilson speaks of evolution through natural selection as a 'natural and spontaneous eugenics' (Gilson 1984: 79). A similar view is expressed by Thomas Nagel, who argues that evolution is directed, ultimately, to the realisation of consciousness – and particularly, consciousness of value. (For Nagel's form of global evolutionary teleology, see Nagel 2012; for a summary of it, see Feser 2019b: 397, 431.) Notably, Nagel – unlike Gilson – has no scholastic or theistic commitments, yet both philosophers endorse a teleological conception of evolution.

may be a profound consonance between natural law teleology and the teleology of evolution. True, human ends or goods are mediated by choice, so are not 'selected' spontaneously; but those who act for their sake are, on this account, acting according to the *nisus* of evolutionary history. It is worth stressing, nonetheless, that this dovetailing between natural law teleology and global evolutionary teleology is not essential to defending the former. Indeed, a far more modest, local teleology is sufficient for that. For irrespective of whether evolution, as a whole, has a direction, it is widely recognised that teleological explanations at a local, viz. functional, level cannot be extruded from the practice of biology.[122] Indeed, long before Darwin, biologists like William Harvey had identified the functions of organs (such as the heart) correctly;[123] and modern biologists, too, regularly pinpoint biological and wider, behavioural, functions without referring to evolutionary history.[124] This bears witness to the distinction between evolutionary and functional biology, two branches of the subject that proceed in substantial practical – yet also logical – independence of each other.[125] As O'Rourke puts things, 'The question of evolution, that is, how form came about historically, is secondary to its role as intrinsic, determining cause of the concrete living beings which we experience here and now'.[126] Just as we can grasp the functioning of the natural elements without knowing their origin or 'descent', so we can grasp the functioning of organs and organisms without knowing theirs.[127] It follows that, once again, evolutionary biology is not a genuine threat to natural law theory. Far from it: if natural law goods like health, reproductive fitness and knowledge are key functional ends of our bodily and cognitive faculties, then evolutionary biology – operating at a local level – does nothing to undermine, and may well facilitate, our identification and understanding of those goods.

---

[122] Gilson argues that teleological (or 'final') explanations are ineliminable from biology (Gilson 1984: 119, 121). Crucially, and in line with Aristotle, he claims they are compatible with material, efficient explanations (p. 112). Yet, equally crucially, the former remain irreducible to the latter.

[123] 'The chief function of the heart', Harvey writes, 'is the transmission and pumping of the blood through the arteries to the extremities of the body' (Harvey 1928: 49).

[124] E.g. 'The Predator Detection hypothesis remains the strongest candidate for the function of stotting [by gazelles]' (Caro 1986: 663); 'other antimalarial genes take over the protective function of the sickle-cell gene in ... other warm parts [of the world]' (Diamond 1994: 83).

[125] For the distinction between evolutionary and functional biology, see (e.g.) Devitt (2008: 353–5) and Feser (2019b: 400–1).

[126] O'Rourke (2004: 30). Cf. Kitcher's (1984) distinction between the history and structure of an organism, or Feser's distinction between organic origin and organic identity (Feser 2015: 44; 2019a: 291–2; 2019b: 400).

[127] See Oderberg (2007: 224).

## 5 'New' Natural Law

I have argued, in fine, that, far from being at war, evolutionary biology and natural teleology present us with a constructive dilemma. *Either* evolutionary biology evinces natural teleology at a global level *or* it relies, pervasively, on teleological descriptions and explanations at a local level. Either way, evolutionary biology and natural law theory are compatible; and, when taken together with evolutionary biology's compatibility with essentialism, the relations between it and natural law look thoroughly eirenic. There remain, nevertheless, parties to the debate who disagree – on both sides. On the natural law side, despair at overcoming *both* the fact/value distinction *and* the supposed rift between evolutionary biology and natural teleology led to the formation of a fresh approach to natural law theory altogether. Known widely as the 'new' natural law theory, it originated with the theologian Germain Grisez in the United States, was given definitive shape by the Oxford jurisprudent John Finnis – in his book *Natural Law and Natural Rights*[128] – and has been honed philosophically by the Toronto-based philosopher Joseph Boyle. Central to their collective project is the idea that natural law theory must no longer appeal – either directly or foundationally – to natural essences-with-ends. Indeed, they deny, in a strongly and explicitly anti-metaphysical vein, that nature (including human nature) is properly a source of norms at all. As Finnis writes,

> the first principles of natural law, which specify the basic forms of good and evil ... are not inferred from facts. They are not inferred from metaphysical propositions about human nature ... or about 'the function of a human being'; nor are they inferred from a teleological conception of nature or any other conception of nature. They are not inferred or derived from anything. (Finnis 2011: 33–4)[129]

This raises the question of how, exactly, Finnis envisages our knowing the first principles of natural law at all. To this he has an ingenious answer.[130]

According to Finnis, it is false that 'for Aquinas "good and evil are concepts analysed and fixed in metaphysics before they are applied in morals" [O'Connor

---

[128] Published originally in 1980, Finnis's book was republished in a second edition in 2011 (see Finnis 2011). I will take it as the paradigm expression of new natural law theory. The latter is summarised helpfully in a joint paper, 'Practical Principles, Moral Truth, and Ultimate Ends' (Finnis et al. 1987). For a very perspicuous introduction to new natural law, see Lee (2019).

[129] Cf. the claim that new natural law 'departs from classical models ... by taking full account of the fact that the moral ought cannot be derived from the is of theoretical truth – for example, of metaphysics and/or philosophical anthropology' (Finnis et al. 1987: 101–2). This indicates, incontrovertibly, that Grisez, Finnis and Boyle accept and place great weight on Hume's inferential argument for the fact/value distinction.

[130] An answer he ascribes often – for all the avowed 'newness' of his theory – to Aquinas. For Finnis's equivocation on the Thomistic credentials of his theory, see Oderberg (2010).

1967: 19]. On the contrary, Aquinas asserts as plainly as possible that the first principles of natural law ... are *per se nota* (self-evident) and indemonstrable ... They are underived (though not innate)' (Finnis 2011: 33–4). This claim of self-evidence and underivedness still leaves open, of course, the epistemic route to grasping these first principles. Finnis's reply is that the route in question is practical reason: 'for Aquinas', he holds,

> the way to discover what is morally right (virtue) and wrong (vice) is to ask, not what is in accordance with human nature, but what is reasonable ... the primary categories for Aquinas are the 'good' and the 'reasonable'; the 'natural' is, from the point of view of his ethics, a speculative appendage added by way of metaphysical reflection, *not* a counter with which to advance either to or from the practical *prima principia per se nota*. (Finnis 2011: 36)

Now Finnis admits (though more or less as an aside) that 'Aquinas would agree that "were man's nature different, so would be his duties"' (Finnis 2011: 34). Yet he insists that this is merely an observation pertinent to the 'ontological order' (Finnis 1983: 21). Epistemically, or in the order of knowledge, 'human nature is not "the basis of ethics"; rather, ethics [*qua* practical reason] is an indispensable preliminary to a full and soundly based knowledge of human nature' (Finnis 1983: 21). As Robert George puts things, interpreting new natural law metaethics: 'in the epistemological mode of inquiry, our (practical) knowledge of human good(s) is methodologically prior to our (speculative) knowledge of human nature. The latter knowledge presupposes the former: It is not, as neo-scholastics suppose, the other way round'. By contrast, however,

> in the ontological mode of inquiry, an account of the human goods will refer back to human nature: 'Why are these the ends fulfilling of human beings?' 'Because human nature is constituted as it is'. But this answer in no way entails that our knowledge of the ends as human fulfilments is derived from prior speculative knowledge of human nature. (George 1988: 1416–17)[131]

In sum, Finnis's view is that normativity (as revealed by practical reason) yields a knowledge of human nature, and not vice versa.[132]

Before interrogating this view, it is worth explicating, in brief, Finnis's understanding of the deliverances of practical reason.[133] For Finnis, practical reason discerns a series of 'basic goods', goods that constitute 'the range of

---

[131] See also Donnelly (2006: 1), Lee (2009) and Oderberg (2010: 67–8).

[132] Cf. Tollefsen (2018: 243–4, 255–6).

[133] Admittedly, this is not straightforward, since the new natural law theory has been developed by a diverse set of scholars and has thus assumed subtly different forms. Mark Murphy and Alfonso Gómez-Lobo, for example, specify 'basic goods' that diverge from Finnis's list (see Murphy 2001: ch. 3 and Gómez-Lobo 2002: ch. 2, respectively.) As I indicated in Note 128, however, I will focus on Finnis's seminal version of the theory.

possibly worthwhile activities and orientations' open to the average moral agent (Finnis 2011: 81). Basic goods are not particular in nature but rather categories of good that are instantiated in any situation of choice. On Finnis's analysis, there are precisely seven such categories: life; knowledge; play; aesthetic experience; sociability or friendship; religion; and practical reasonableness.[134] These seven basic goods are, importantly, 'pre-moral', in the sense that – even once one has identified those relevant to a particular situation of deliberative choice – they are not sufficient *per se* to determine that choice. Moral choice, properly so-called, must abide, in addition, by practically rational norms, which select and arrange the goods in question. Practically rational norms include the principle that there be no arbitrary preferences between persons; that there be respect for every basic value in every act; and that the basic goods chosen should contribute to a coherent plan of life.[135] Practically rational choice further requires the recognition that the basic goods are incommensurable, since, according to new natural law, there is no common scale or measure by which particular instantiations of those goods can be aggregated. Indeed, if there were such a scale, then all moral choice would amount to no more than a summing of quantities – thereby denying, in effect, the substantive, relatively open, nature of such choice.[136] Rather, practically rational choice is guided essentially and properly by the life plans of particular agents.[137]

With this outline in place, it is plain that Finnis has arrogated extensive and significant powers to practical reason. It delivers knowledge not only of the basic categories of human good but also of those principles that undergird moral choice. In this way, it is freighted with both strong welfarist and strong moral powers. True, Finnis's talk of indemonstrability and self-evidence suggests an a prioristic view of the basic goods, which do not admit, it seems, of any explication or justification.[138] Yet this impression is questionable. In point of fact, Finnis's claims of self-evidence and indemonstrability do not preclude support for the basic goods. As he writes, invoking Aquinas, there can be '"induction" of indemonstrable first principles of practical reason (i.e. of natural law) by insight working on felt inclinations and a knowledge of possibilities';[139] and he grants that 'anthropological and psychological studies' constitute 'an

---

[134] See Finnis (2011: ch. 4). Since the 1990s, several new natural law theorists have argued that marriage is a distinct basic good. (Marriage is one of the human goods Aquinas mentions at *Summa Theologiae* I–II, 94.2.)

[135] For further examples and analysis, see Finnis (2011: ch. 5).

[136] A corollary of this is that new natural law is firmly anti-consequentialist. See, for example, Grisez (1978) and Finnis (2011: 111–18).

[137] For criticism of this 'agent-centred' rather than 'world-centred' approach to moral choice, see (e.g.) MacIntyre (2000) and Oderberg (2010: 46–7).

[138] For this view, see Haldane (2013). [139] Finnis (2011: 77). Cf. Finnis (1981: 268).

assemblage of reminders of the range of possibly worthwhile activities and orientations open to one'.[140] So one cannot fault new natural law along quite these lines. Likewise, I want to bracket two further avenues of criticism, namely, first, that Finnis's theory is not faithful to Aquinas,[141] and secondly, that its list of basic goods is somehow too long, too short, or otherwise open to objection.[142] The first criticism is primarily of historical interest, while the second, like the first, is not directly relevant to what is, in this context, the key question – viz. how, exactly, is new natural law *natural*? For it is one thing to claim that certain basic goods and practical principles recommend themselves to practical reason; it is quite another to show that practical reason is responding here to what nature requires, or to what are, put otherwise, natural ends or *telē*.

In response to this question, traditional natural lawyers – viz. those who never recognised the need for 'new' natural law and repudiate its explicit 'metaphysicophobia'[143] – have been relentlessly critical. According to Ralph McInerny, for instance, new natural law is simply 'natural law without nature'.[144] For Oderberg,

> What is troubling about [the new natural law] position is the interpretation of theoretical and metaphysical truth . . . that derives directly from the Humean, positivistic approach to facts and values . . . [Without] addressing . . . basic ontological questions about the nature of reality, nonhuman as well as human . . . natural law theory risks floating free of substantive moorings and acquiring an excessively subjective and first-personal methodology. (Oderberg 2010: 47)

To be fair, Finnis steers clear of an estrangement between practical reason and nature that is absolute. One needs, he maintains, 'theoretical knowledge about one's own powers . . . to know what one might choose to do',[145] while the 'possibility of human fulfilment', he holds, 'presupposes . . . the given reality of human nature – with its capacities and inclinations . . . what still can be presupposes what already is; in particular, what one naturally is grounds all that one is to be'.[146] In this way, Finnis suggests what Mark Murphy calls a 'weak grounding' of the basic goods in human nature.[147] These goods are not derived from human nature by deduction – in this sense, they are, indeed, 'indemonstrable' – but human nature still constitutes the background against which they are

---

[140] Finnis (2011: 81).

[141] For this view, see McInerny (1982); Hittinger (1987); Lisska (1996); Seagrave (2009); Oderberg (2010); Pakaluk (2013).

[142] For this type of view, see Anderson (2005), Dubois (2006) and Crisp (2013).

[143] To redeploy Rommen's term – see Note 35.       [144] Quoted in Feser (2019a: 276).

[145] Finnis et al. (1987: 111).       [146] Finnis et al. (1987: 116).       [147] See Murphy (2001: 15).

intelligible *qua* goods; and this reflects Finnis's view that, though *epistemically* what is good for us does not depend on human nature – for this would constitute, recalling Hume's inferential argument, 'derivationism' – *ontologically* what is good for us does depend on our nature.[148] In this way, Finnis's position may, after all, be genuinely naturalistic and thus continuous with traditional natural law: if, that is, this 'weak' form of grounding is adequate.[149]

A note of severe caution is, however, in order, for not all new natural lawyers appear to allow even weak grounding of the basic goods in human nature. Christopher Tollefsen, for example, argues that 'the goods known in the third [practical] order are fulfilments of human nature *in that order*, and not in the first [natural] order';[150] and this because 'our biological species life does not ... seem to possess any straightforward normativity for us'.[151] In other words, the basic goods cannot be fulfilments of human nature *simpliciter*, because the latter is not intrinsically teleological; it is, at most, a *mélange* of drives and potentialities, which have no distinct practical or moral shape until practical reason intervenes to supply these.[152] Yet this elevation of the 'practical' into an 'order' of its own looks, for traditional natural law, like an illegitimate and mystifying hypostatisation. If Tollefsen is right, and the basic goods are grounded not in the natural order *stricto sensu* but only in a hypostatised practical order, then new natural law – as genuinely and discernibly *natural* – will struggle to escape the charge of being, itself, illegitimate and mystifying.[153]

## 6 Prospective Conclusion

I began by outlining the history of natural law theory, which, although it has substantial roots in Plato and Aristotle, comes to self-consciousness, as it were, only with the Stoics and Aquinas. I then went on to document two modes of natural law thought – social contractarian and 'theological unificationist' –

---

[148] See Finnis (1987, 1998: 90–4. The term 'derivationism' is Murphy's. See Murphy (2001: ch. 1, § 1).

[149] Peter Seipel argues that, by abandoning derivationism, Finnis is also abandoning authentic natural law. See Seipel (2015).

[150] Tollefsen (2018: 245).     [151] Tollefsen (2018: 253).

[152] NB 'first order nature contains potentialities and actualities that are not and never will be realised by intelligible basic goods: potentialities clearly rooted in our animal nature to hurt, destroy, dominate, and the like ... and potentialities that are simply neutral' (Tollefsen 2018: 256).

[153] In posing this challenge to new natural lawyers, I do not mean to suggest they cannot meet it. After all, they claim to have elaborated a genuinely *natural* law theory, albeit one that is new in some respects (e.g. in its doctrine of incommensurability, its strong distinction between epistemic and ontological 'orders' and, arguably, its embrace of the modern idiom of 'human rights'). Indeed, the practical deliverances of new natural law dovetail quite extensively with those of traditional natural law; and, in this respect, at least, new natural law appears strongly continuous with its traditional counterpart.

which are tangential to, and incompatible with, the core tradition. With this historical ballast in place, I elaborated a substantive philosophical method, which has strong echoes in political philosophy, namely the *via negativa* of uncovering 'manifest injustice'. This method assumes that we can discern natural law norms most readily when they are contravened. Drawing on both Sophocles' play *Antigone* and the actual case of Josef Fritzl, I upheld a paradigm set of natural law norms, which reflect a basically Aristotelian philosophical anthropology. I then deepened my exploration of natural law theory with two, seminal, challenges to its methodology: the fact/value distinction in metaethics, on the one hand, and evolutionary biology, on the other. I argued that neither of these challenges is devastating, even though both are significant and need, certainly, to be taken seriously. Finally, I rounded off my investigation with a look at 'new' natural law, a theory which is markedly concessive toward – yet also designed to bypass – the two challenges immediately above. While Finnis's theory is intriguing and intellectually impressive, its strong reliance on a substantially autonomous practical reason departs from traditional natural law, since it makes at best only an oblique appeal to the norms of nature. Whether it counts, strictly, as a *natural* law theory is, therefore, open to real doubt.

All in all, I hope I have (at least) kept the threats to natural law theory at bay and (at most) shown it to be a lively and promising source of ethical reflection, whose determination to keep the normative grounded in the natural is both theoretically indispensable and practically timely. Ethical theory's 'metaphysicophobia' may still be prevalent, at least in anglophone analytic moral philosophy, but it is long past its use-by date. It is time that ethics returned home – namely, to an unpacking of the human essence and its manifold ends. Given that no less a moral philosopher than Terence Irwin has made this clarion call in a work of great depth and breadth,[154] I think the prospects of its being heeded are brighter, perhaps, than at any point since the seventeenth century. If my small contribution adds to that brightness somewhat, my job will have been done – if only by pointing to where the true light shines.

---

[154] See *The Development of Ethics*, a study in three volumes (Irwin 2011).

# References

Alford, C. F. (2010). *Narrative, Nature, and the Natural Law: From Aquinas to International Human Rights*. Basingstoke: Palgrave Macmillan.

Andersen, S. (2001). 'Theological Ethics, Moral Philosophy, and Natural Law', *Ethical Theory and Moral Practice* 4 (December), 349–64. https://doi.org/10.1023/A:1013318824823.

Anderson, O. (2005). 'Is Contemporary Natural Law Theory a Beneficial Development? The Attempt to Study Natural Law and the Human Good without Metaphysics', *New Blackfriars* 86 (1005), 478–92. https://doi.org/10.1111/j.0028-4289.2005.00102.x.

Angier, T. (2019). 'Two Dogmas of (Modern) Aristotle Scholarship', *Dialogoi: Ancient Philosophy Today* 1 (2), 237–55. https://doi.org/10.3366/anph.2019.0017.

Aquinas (2006). *Summa Theologiae*, trans. Fathers of the English Dominican Province. Cambridge: Cambridge University Press. [Complete English edition]

Aristotle (1984). *The Complete Words of Aristotle*, ed. Jonathan Barnes. Princeton: Princeton University Press. [Revised Oxford translation]

Ayala, F. J. (1970). 'Teleological Explanations in Evolutionary Biology', *Philosophy of Science* 37 (1): 1–15.

Barney, R. (2006). 'The Sophistic Movement'. In M. L. Gill and P. Pellegrin, eds, *A Companion to Ancient Philosophy*. Oxford: Wiley-Blackwell, pp. 77–97.

Bedau, M. (1992). 'Where's the Good in Teleology?' *Philosophy and Phenomenological Research* 52 (4), 781–806. https://doi.org/10.2307/2107911.

Boyd, R. (1999). 'Homeostasis, Species, and Higher Taxa'. In Robert Wilson, ed., *Species: New Interdisciplinary Essays*. Cambridge: Cambridge University Press, pp. 141–85.

Braithwaite, R. B. (1946). 'Teleological Explanation', *Proceedings of the Aristotelian Society (New Series)* 47, i–xx.

Brüllmann, P. (2019). 'The Stoics'. In T. Angier, ed., *The Cambridge Companion to Natural Law Ethics*. Cambridge: Cambridge University Press, pp. 11–30.

Caro, T. M. (1986). 'The Functions of Stotting in Thomson's Gazelles: Some Tests of the Predictions', *Animal Behaviour* 34 (3), 663–84. https://doi.org/10.1016/S0003-3472(86)80052-5.

Chappell, S. G. (2017). 'The Objectivity of Ordinary Life', *Ethical Theory and Moral Practice* 20 (4), 709–21. https://doi.org/10.1007/s10677-017-9793-2.

Cicero (1998). *The Republic and The Laws*, trans. N. Rudd. Oxford: Oxford University Press.

Cohen, G. A. (1989). 'On the Currency of Egalitarian Justice', *Ethics* 99 (4), 906–44. https://doi.org/10.1086/293126.

Crisp, R. (2013). 'Finnis on Well-Being'. In J. Keown and R. P. George, eds, *Reason, Morality, and Law: The Philosophy of John Finnis*. Oxford: Oxford University Press, pp. 24–36.

Crowe, M. B. (1977). *The Changing Profile of the Natural Law*. The Hague: Martinus Nijhoff.

Cuneo, T. (2007). *The Normative Web: An Argument for Moral Realism*. Oxford: Oxford University Press.

Darwin, C. ([1858] 1996). *The Origin of Species*. Oxford: Oxford University Press.

Depew, D. J. (2008). 'Consequence Etiology and Biological Teleology in Aristotle and Darwin', *Studies in History and Philosophy of Science* 39 (4), 379–90. https://doi.org/10.1016/j.shpsc.2008.09.001.

De Queiroz, K. (1999). 'The General Lineage Concept of Species and the Defining Properties of the Species Category'. In Robert Wilson, ed., *Species: New Interdisciplinary Essays*. Cambridge: Cambridge University Press, pp. 49–89.

Deslauriers, M. (2003). 'Aristotle on the Virtues of Slaves and Women', *Oxford Studies in Ancient Philosophy* 25 (Winter), 213–31.

Devitt, M. (2008). 'Resurrecting Biological Essentialism', *Philosophy of Science* 75 (3), 344–82. https://doi.org/10.1086/593566.

Diamond, J. (1994). 'Race without Color', *Discover Magazine* 15 (11), 82–6.

Di Blasi, F. (2006). *God and the Natural Law: A Rereading of Thomas Aquinas*. South Bend, IN: St Augustine's Press.

Donnelly, B. (2006). 'The Epistemic Connection between Nature and Value in New and Traditional Natural Law Theory', *Law and Philosophy* 25 (1), 1–29. https://doi.org/10.1007/s 10982-004-5055-2 29.

Dubois, J. M. (2006). 'How Much Guidance Can a Secular, Natural Law Ethic Offer? A Study of Basic Human Goods in Ethical Decision-Making'. In M. J. Cherry, ed., *The Death of Metaphysics; The Death of Culture: Epistemology, Metaphysics and Morality*. Dordrecht: Springer, pp. 185–97.

Dupré, J. (1999). 'On the Impossibility of a Monistic Account of Species'. In Robert Wilson (ed.), *Species: New Interdisciplinary Essays*. Cambridge: Cambridge University Press, pp. 3–22.

Ellis, B. (2001). *Scientific Essentialism*. Cambridge: Cambridge University Press.

Emon, A. (2019). 'Natural Law in Islam'. In T. Angier, ed., *The Cambridge Companion to Natural Law Ethics*. Cambridge: Cambridge University Press, pp. 179–96.

Feser, E. (2014). *Scholastic Metaphysics: A Contemporary Introduction*. Heusenstamm: Editiones Scholasticae.

Feser, E. (2015). 'Teleology: A Shopper's Guide'. In E. Feser, *Neo-Scholastic Essays*. South Bend, IN: St Augustine's Press, pp. 28–48.

Feser, E. (2019a). 'Natural Law Ethics and the Revival of Aristotelian Metaphysics'. In T. Angier, ed., *The Cambridge Companion to Natural Law Ethics*. Cambridge: Cambridge University Press, pp. 276–96.

Feser, E. (2019b). *Aristotle's Revenge: The Metaphysical Foundations of Physical and Biological Science*. Heusenstamm: Editiones Scholasticae.

Finnis, J. (1981). 'Natural Law and the "Is"-"Ought" Question: An Invitation to Professor Veatch', *Catholic Lawyer* 26 (4), 266–77.

Finnis, J. (1983). *Fundamentals of Ethics*. Washington, DC: University of Georgetown Press.

Finnis, J. (1987). 'Natural Inclinations and Natural Rights: Deriving "Ought" from "Is" According to Aquinas'. In L. J. Elders and K. Hedwig, eds, *Lex et Libertas: Freedom and Law according to St. Thomas Aquinas*, vol. 30. Rome: Studi Tomistici.

Finnis, J. (1998). *Aquinas: Moral, Political, and Legal Theory*. Oxford: Oxford University Press.

Finnis, J. ([1980] 2011). *Natural Law and Natural Rights*, 2nd ed. Oxford: Oxford University Press.

Finnis, J., Grisez, G. and Boyle, J. (1987). 'Practical Principles, Moral Truth, and Ultimate Ends', *The American Journal of Jurisprudence* 32 (1), 99–151.

Frankena, W. K. (1939). 'The Naturalistic Fallacy', *Mind* (New Series), 48 (192), 464–77.

George, R. P. (1988). 'Recent Criticism of Natural Law Theory', *University of Chicago Law Review* 55 (4), 1371–429.

Gilson, E. (1984). *From Aristotle to Darwin and Back Again: A Journey in Final Causality, Species, and Evolution*. Notre Dame, IN: University of Notre Dame Press.

Gómez-Lobo, A. (2002). *Morality and the Human Goods: An Introduction to Natural Law Ethics*. Washington, DC: Georgetown University Press.

Goyette, J., Latkovic, M. S. and Myers, R. S. (2004). *St. Thomas Aquinas and the Natural Law Tradition: Contemporary Perspectives*. Washington, DC: The Catholic University of America Press.

Griffiths, P. (2002). 'What Is Innateness?', *Monist* 85 (1), 70–85. https://doi.org/10.5840/monist20028518.

Grisez, G. (1965). 'The First Principle of Practical Reason: A Commentary on the *Summa Theologiae*, 1–2, Question 94, Article 2', *The American Journal of Jurisprudence* 10 (1), 168–201.

Grisez, G. (1978). 'Against Consequentialism', *The American Journal of Jurisprudence* 23 (1), 21–72.

Guthrie, W. K. C. (1981). *History of Philosophy, Vol. 6: Aristotle: An Encounter.* Cambridge: Cambridge University Press.

Haakonssen, K. (2008). 'Natural Law without Metaphysics: A Protestant Tradition'. In A. M. González, ed., *Contemporary Perspectives on Natural Law: Natural Law As a Limiting Concept.* London: Ashgate Publishing, pp. 67–86.

Haldane, J. (2013). 'Reasoning About the Human Good, and the Role of the Public Philosopher'. In J. Keown and R. P. George, eds, *Reason, Morality, and Law: The Philosophy of John Finnis.* Oxford: Oxford University Press, pp. 37–55.

Hampshire, S. (2000). *Justice Is Conflict.* Princeton: Princeton University Press.

Harvey, W. ([1616] 1928). *Exercitatio anatomica de motu cordis et sanguinis in animalibus*, trans. C. Depew Leake. Baltimore, MD: Charles C. Thomas.

Hawthorne, J. and Nolan, D. (2006). 'What Would Teleological Causation Be?' In J. Hawthorne, *Metaphysical Essays.* Oxford: Clarendon Press, pp. 265–84.

Heath, M. (2008). 'Aristotle on Natural Slavery', *Phronesis* 53 (3), 243–70. https://doi.org/10.1163/156852808X307070.

Hegel, G. W. F. (1977). *The Phenomenology of Spirit*, trans. A. V. Miller. Oxford: Oxford University Press.

Hittinger, R. (1987). *A Critique of the New Natural Law Theory.* Notre Dame, IN: University of Notre Dame Press.

Hume, D. (1998). *An Enquiry Concerning the Principles of Morals.* Oxford: Oxford University Press.

Hume, D. (2007). *A Treatise of Human Nature*, vol. 1. Oxford: Oxford University Press.

Hüntelmann, R. (2016). *Grundkurs Philosophie, Vol. 6: Natürliche Ethik.* Heusenstamm: Editiones Scholasticae.

Hurka, T. (2001). *Virtue, Vice, and Value.* Oxford: Oxford University Press.

Inwood, B. and Gerson, L. P. (1997). *Hellenistic Philosophy: Introductory Readings.* Indianapolis, IN: Hackett Publishing.

Inwood, B. and Gerson, L. P. (2008). *The Stoics Reader: Selected Writings and Testimonia.* Indianapolis, IN: Hackett Publishing.

Irwin, T. (2011). *The Development of Ethics*, 3 vols. Oxford: Oxford University Press.

Jensen, S. J. (2015). *Knowing the Natural Law: From Precepts and Inclinations to Deriving Oughts*. Washington, DC: The Catholic University of America Press.

Jensen, S. J. (2019). 'Aquinas'. In T. Angier, ed., *The Cambridge Companion to Natural Law Ethics*. Cambridge: Cambridge University Press, pp. 31–50.

Kelsen, H. (1960). 'Plato and the Doctrine of Natural Law', *Vanderbilt Law Review* 14 (1), 23–64.

Kirchin, S. (2013). *Thick Concepts*. Oxford: Oxford University Press.

Kitcher, P. (1984). 'Species', *Philosophy of Science* 51 (2), 308–333. https://doi.org/10.1086/289182.

Klein, J. (2012). 'Stoic Eudaimonism and the Natural Law Tradition'. In J. A. Jacobs, ed., *Reason, Religion, and Natural Law: From Plato to Spinoza*. Oxford: Oxford University Press, pp. 57–80.

Lee, P. (2009). 'Human Nature and Moral Goodness'. In M. J. Cherry, ed., *The Normativity of the Natural: Human Goods, Human Virtues, and Human Flourishing*. Dordrecht: Springer, pp. 45–54.

Lee, P. (2019). 'The New Natural Law Theory'. In T. Angier, ed., *The Cambridge Companion to Natural Law Ethics*. Cambridge: Cambridge University Press, pp. 173–91.

Leiter, B. (2002). *Routledge Philosophy Guidebook to Nietzsche on Morality*. London: Routledge.

Lennox, J. G. (1993). 'Darwin Was a Teleologist', *Biology and Philosophy* 8 (4), 409–21. https://doi.org/10.1007/BF00857687.

Leunissen, M. (2017). *From Natural Character to Moral Virtue in Aristotle*. Oxford: Oxford University Press.

Levering, M. (2008). *Biblical Natural Law: A Theocentric and Teleological Approach*. Oxford: Oxford University Press.

Lewens, T. (2004). *Organisms and Artifacts: Design in Nature and Elsewhere*. Cambridge, MA: MIT Press.

Lewens, T. (2007). *Darwin*. Abingdon: Routledge.

Lisska, A. J. (1996). *Aquinas's Theory of Natural Law: An Analytic Reconstruction*. Oxford: Clarendon Press.

Long, A. A. and Sedley, D. N. (1987). *The Hellenistic Philosophers*, vol. 1. Cambridge: Cambridge University Press.

MacIntyre, A. C. (2000). 'Theories of Natural Law in the Cultures of Advanced Modernity'. In E. B. McLean, ed., *Common Truths: New Perspectives on Natural Law*. Wilmington, DE: ISI Books, pp. 91–115.

Mackie, J. L. (1977). *Ethics: Inventing Right and Wrong*. Harmondsworth: Penguin Books.

Manent, P. (2018). *La loi naturelle et les droits de l'homme*. Paris: Presses Universitaires de France.

Maritain, J. (2001). *Natural Law: Reflections on Theory and Practice*. South Bend, IN: St Augustine's Press.

Marsh, S. and Pancevski, B. (2009). *The Crimes of Josef Fritzl: Uncovering the Truth*. London: HarperElement.

Martin, C. (2004). 'The Fact/Value Distinction'. In T. Chappell and D. S. Oderberg, eds, *Human Values: New Essays on Ethics and Natural Law*. Basingstoke: Palgrave Macmillan, pp. 52–69.

Martin, C. (2008). 'The Relativity of Goodness: A Prolegomenon to a Rapprochement between Virtue Ethics and Natural Law Theory'. In A. M. González, ed., *Contemporary Perspectives on Natural Law: Natural Law As a Limiting Concept*. London: Ashgate Publishing, pp. 187–200.

Mayr, E. (1992). 'Species Concepts and Their Application'. In M. Ereshefsky, ed., *The Units of Evolution: Essays on the Nature of Species*. Cambridge, MA: MIT Press, pp. 15–25.

McInerny, R. M. (1982). *Ethica Thomistica: The Moral Philosophy of Thomas Aquinas*. Washington, DC: The Catholic University of America Press.

Mill, J. S. (1985). *On Liberty*. Harmondsworth: Penguin Books.

Mirus, C. (2004). 'The Metaphysical Roots of Aristotle's Teleology', *The Review of Metaphysics* 57 (4), 699–724. https://doi.org/revmetaph2004 57443.

Mirus, C. (2012). 'Aristotle on Beauty and Goodness in Nature', *International Philosophical Quarterly* 52 (1), 79–97. https://doi.org/10.5840 /ipq20125216.

Monden, L. (1966). *Sin, Liberty and Law*, trans. D. Donceel. London: Geoffrey Chapman.

Moore, G. E. (1903). *Principia Ethica*. Cambridge: Cambridge University Press.

Murphy, M. C. (2001). *Natural Law and Practical Rationality*. Cambridge: Cambridge University Press.

Nagel, T. (2012). *Mind and Cosmos: Why the Materialist Neo-Darwinian Conception of Nature Is Almost Certainly False*. Oxford: Oxford University Press.

Novak, D. (1998). *Natural Law in Judaism*. Cambridge: Cambridge University Press.

Novak, D. (2014). *Natural Law: A Jewish, Christian, and Islamic Trialogue*. Oxford: Oxford University Press.

Nuccetelli, S. and Seay, G. (2012). *Ethical Naturalism: Current Debates*. Cambridge: Cambridge University Press.

O'Connor, D. J. (1967). *Aquinas and Natural Law*. London: Macmillan and Co.

Oderberg, D. S. (2000). *Moral Theory: A Non-Consequentialist Approach*. Oxford: Blackwell Publishers.

Oderberg, D. S. (2004). 'The Structure and Content of the Good'. In T. Chappell and D. S. Oderberg, eds, *Human Values: New Essays on Ethics and Natural Law*. Basingstoke: Palgrave Macmillan, pp. 127–65.

Oderberg, D. S. (2007). *Real Essentialism*. Abingdon: Routledge.

Oderberg, D. S. (2008). 'Teleology: Organic and Inorganic'. In A. M. González, ed., *Contemporary Perspectives on Natural Law: Natural Law As a Limiting Concept*. Aldershot: Ashgate Publishing, pp. 259–80.

Oderberg, D. S. (2010). 'The Metaphysical Foundations of Natural Law'. In H. Zaborowski, ed., *Natural Moral Law in Contemporary Society*. Washington, DC: The Catholic University of America Press, pp. 44–75.

Oderberg, D. S. (2013). 'Natural Law and Rights Theory'. In G. F. Gaus and F. d'Agostino, eds, *The Routledge Companion to Social and Political Philosophy*. Abingdon: Routledge, pp. 375–86.

Oderberg, D. S. (2020). *The Metaphysics of Good and Evil*. Abingdon: Routledge.

Okasha, S. (2002). 'Darwinian Metaphysics: Species and the Question of Essentialism', *Synthèse* 131, 191–213. https://doi.org/10.1023/A:1015731 831011.

O'Rourke, F. (2004). 'Aristotle and the Metaphysics of Evolution'. *The Review of Metaphysics* 58 (1), 3–59. https://doi.org/revmetaph200458181.

Pakaluk, M. (2013). 'Is the New Natural Law Thomistic?' *The National Catholic Bioethics Quarterly* 13 (1), 57–67. https://doi.org/10.5840/ncbq201313170.

Plato (1997). *Complete Works*, ed. J. M. Cooper and D. S. Hutchinson. Indianapolis, IN: Hackett Publishing.

Porter, J. (1999). *Natural and Divine Law: Reclaiming the Tradition for Christian Ethics*. Grand Rapids, MI: W. B. Eerdmans Publishing.

Porter, J. (2005). *Nature As Reason: A Thomistic Theory of the Natural Law*. Grand Rapids, MI: W. B. Eerdmans Publishing.

Porter, J. (2009). 'Does the Natural Law Provide a Universally Valid Morality?'. In L. S. Cunningham, ed., *Intractable Disputes about the Natural Law: Alasdair MacIntyre and His Critics*. Notre Dame, IN: University of Notre Dame Press, pp. 53–95.

Putnam, H. (2002). *The Collapse of the Fact/Value Dichotomy and Other Essays*. Cambridge, MA: Harvard University Press.

Putnam, H. (2017). 'The Fact/Value Dichotomy and the Future of Philosophy'. In G. Marchetti and S. Marchetti, eds, *Facts and Values: The Ethics and Metaphysics of Normativity*. Abingdon: Routledge, pp. 27–41.

Rapp, C. (2016). '"Der Staat existiert von Natur aus": Über eine befremdliche These im ersten Buch der Aristotelischen Politik'. In A. Höfele and B. Kellner, eds, *Menschennatur und Politische Ordnung*. Paderborn: Wilhelm Fink, pp. 45–78.

Rommen, H. A. (1998). *The Natural Law: A Study in Legal and Social History and Philosophy*. Indianapolis, IN: Liberty Fund.

Rosenberg, A. (1985). *The Structure of Biological Science*. New York: Cambridge University Press.

Rowland, T. (2019). 'Natural Law in Catholic Christianity'. In T. Angier, ed., *The Cambridge Companion to Natural Law Ethics*. Cambridge: Cambridge University Press, pp. 135–54.

Rudavsky, T. (2019). 'Natural Law in Judaism'. In T. Angier, ed., *The Cambridge Companion to Natural Law Ethics*. Cambridge: Cambridge University Press, pp. 113–34.

Seagrave, S. A. (2009). 'Cicero, Aquinas, and Contemporary Issues in Natural Law Theory', *The Review of Metaphysics* 62 (3), 491–523. https://doi.org /revmetaph20096231.

Searle, J. R. (1964). 'How to Derive "Ought" From "Is"', *The Philosophical Review* 73 (1), 43–58.

Seipel, P. (2015). 'Aquinas and the Natural Law: A Derivationist Reading of ST I-II, Q. 94, A. 2', *Journal of Religious Ethics* 43 (1), 28–50. https://doi.org/10 .1111/jore.12085.

Sen, A. (2009). *The Idea of Justice*. London: Penguin Books.

Simon, Y. R. (1965). *The Tradition of Natural Law: A Philosopher's Reflections*. New York: Fordham University Press.

Simpson, P. P. (2001). *Vices, Virtues, and Consequences: Essays in Moral and Political Philosophy*. Washington, DC: The Catholic University of America Press.

Sober, E. (1992). 'Evolution, Population Thinking and Essentialism', *Philosophy of Science* 47, 350–83. Reprinted in M. Ereshefsky, ed., *The Units of Evolution: Essays on the Nature of Species*. Cambridge, MA: MIT Press, pp. 247–78.

Solinas, M. (2015). *From Aristotle's Teleology to Darwin's Genealogy: The Stamp of Inutility*. Basingstoke: Palgrave Macmillan.

Sophocles (1954). *Sophocles I: Oedipus the King; Oedipus at Colonus; Antigone*. Chicago: University of Chicago Press.

Spaemann, R. (2008). 'The Unrelinquishability of Teleology'. In A. M. González, ed., *Contemporary Perspectives on Natural Law: Natural Law As a Limiting Concept*. Aldershot: Ashgate Publishing, pp. 281–96.

Tollefsen, C. (2018). 'Aquinas's Four Orders, Normativity, and Human Nature', *The Journal of Value Inquiry* 52 (3), 243–56. https://doi.org/10.1007/S10790-018-9657-6.

Tolstoy, L. (2000). *Anna Karenina*. London: Penguin Books.

Toner, C. (2008). 'Sorts of Naturalism: Requirements for a Successful Theory', *Metaphilosophy* 39 (2), 220–50. https://doi.org/10.1111/j.1467-9973.2008.00538.x.

Vavova, K. (2015). 'Evolutionary Debunking of Moral Realism', *Philosophy Compass* 10 (2), 104–16. https://doi.org/10.1111/phc3.12194.

Veatch, H. B. (1966). 'Non-Cognitivism in Ethics: A Modest Proposal for its Diagnosis and Cure', *Ethics* 76 (2), 102–16.

Veatch, H. B. (2003). *Rational Man: A Modern Interpretation of Aristotelian Ethics*. Washington, DC: The Catholic University of America Press.

Wild, J. (1953). *Plato's Modern Enemies and the Theory of Natural Law*. Chicago: Chicago University Press.

Wildes, K. W. (2006). 'Whose Nature? Natural Law in a Pluralistic World'. In M. J. Cherry, ed., *The Death of Metaphysics; The Death of Culture: Epistemology, Metaphysics and Morality*. Dordrecht: Springer, pp. 31–40.

Williams, B. A. O. (1995). 'Evolution, Ethics, and the Representation Problem'. In B. A. O. Williams, *Making Sense of Humanity*. Cambridge: Cambridge University Press, pp. 100–10.

Williams, B. A. O. (2003). 'Plato's Construction of Intrinsic Goodness'. In R. W. Sharples, ed., *Perspectives on Greek Philosophy: S. V. Keeling Memorial Lectures in Ancient Philosophy 1991–2002*. Ashgate Keeling Series in Ancient Philosophy. Aldershot: Ashgate Publishing, pp. 1–18.

Wolff, J. (2015). 'Social Equality and Social Inequality'. In C. Fourie, F. Schuppert and I. Wallimann-Helmer, eds, *Social Equality: On What It Means to Be Equals*. Oxford: Oxford University Press, pp. 209–25.

Cambridge Elements ≡

# Ethics

## Ben Eggleston

*University of Kansas*

Ben Eggleston is a professor of philosophy at the University of Kansas. He is the editor of *John Stuart Mill, Utilitarianism: With Related Remarks from Mill's Other Writings* (Hackett, 2017) and a co-editor of *Moral Theory and Climate Change: Ethical Perspectives on a Warming Planet* (Routledge, 2020), *The Cambridge Companion to Utilitarianism* (Cambridge, 2014), and *John Stuart Mill and the Art of Life* (Oxford, 2011). He is also the author of numerous articles and book chapters on various topics in ethics.

## Dale E. Miller

*Old Dominion University, Virginia*

Dale E. Miller is a professor of philosophy at Old Dominion University. He is the author of *John Stuart Mill: Moral, Social and Political Thought* (Polity, 2010) and a co-editor of *Moral Theory and Climate Change: Ethical Perspectives on a Warming Planet* (Routledge, 2020), *A Companion to Mill* (Blackwell, 2017), *The Cambridge Companion to Utilitarianism* (Cambridge, 2014), *John Stuart Mill and the Art of Life* (Oxford, 2011), and *Morality, Rules, and Consequences: A Critical Reader* (Edinburgh, 2000). He is also the editor-in-chief of *Utilitas*, and the author of numerous articles and book chapters on various topics in ethics broadly construed.

## About the Series

This Elements series provides an extensive overview of major figures, theories, and concepts in the field of ethics. Each entry in the series acquaints students with the main aspects of its topic while articulating the author's distinctive viewpoint in a manner that will interest researchers.

## Cambridge Elements ⹀

# Ethics

### Elements in the Series

*Contractualism*
Jussi Suikkanen

*Epistemology and Methodology in Ethics*
Tristram McPherson

*Ethical Subjectivism and Expressivism*
Neil Sinclair

*Thomas Reid on the Ethical Life*
Terence Cuneo

*Moore's Ethics*
William H. Shaw

*Contemporary Virtue Ethics*
Nancy E. Snow

*Morality and Practical Reasons*
Douglas W. Portmore

*Subjective versus Objective Moral Wrongness*
Peter A. Graham

*Parfit's Ethics*
Richard Yetter Chappell

*Moral Psychology*
Christian B. Miller

*Philippa Foot's Metaethics*
John Hacker-Wright

*Natural Law Theory*
Tom Angier

A full series listing is available at www.cambridge.org/EETH

Printed in the United States
by Baker & Taylor Publisher Services